EMPATH

Empowering Highly Sensitive People - Maximizing Your Potential and Self-Awareness

CALEB BENSON

Contents

Introduction

Does being in public places sometimes overwhelm you due to over-stimulation? Do you have an uncanny knack for detecting lies? Maybe you've noticed that you developed sympathy symptoms from someone else's ailments or find that others tend to always unload their problems on you. Are you drawn to metaphysical healing and the supernatural in general? If you answered yes to any of these questions, you may be realizing that you are an Empath! As an Empath, you absorb both the emotions and feelings of other people as if they were your own. Because Empaths are typically so compassionate, intuitive, loving, and insightful, they can focus so much on the needs of others that they sometimes disregard their own.

Empaths can read what others are feeling and resonate them on a level unknown to most people. If you can do this, you are in a growing community of people that are now embracing and using these abilities as a gift in the healing of themselves and others. This feeling of being "in-tune" to the sensitivities of others happens not only with friend and family but with complete strangers, too! Empaths tend to be hyper-sensitive when it comes to smell, sound, light, taste, touch, and it usually extends to their emotional natures as well.

Empaths can't help noticing that some things are different for them. In the end, it's usually through someone else's description of their experience, that empaths finally exclaim: "That's exactly how I feel!" It can be extremely validating for a novice to realize that there are others that feel and experience the world in the same ways that they do.

In this book, we will explore the Science behind Empathy. Are we genetically predisposed for empathy, and can it be learned later in life? We'll discover the Neuroscience behind Mirror Neurons and the Electro-magnetic fields of humans. Knowing the biology responsible for your condition and abilities can help when determining how you will practice and enhance your ability. We also will dive into the types of sensitivities commonly found in Empaths so that you can determine where you are able to use your empathy for the good of others, and where you need to beware of overextending yourself.

There are many challenges that come along with this newfound awareness of being an Empath. Learn about how being an Empath will affect the many aspects of daily life including how you will affect others. Accepting your gift and finding balance in your life will be crucial. Release negative energy through balancing your Chakras and practicing Yoga. Learn tips for empowering yourself and finding a community of support on your journey to self-awareness.

Finally, we explore techniques for grounding yourself and blocking out the unwanted emotions and energies of others. Setting your energetic boundaries and avoiding burnout through honoring who you are and nurturing your empathic abilities. Learn about the different types of emotions so that you are prepared to deal with them when they catch you off guard.

Am I an Empath?

I f you feel that you may be an Empath, you probably are one! Most people have a certain level of sensitivity when it comes to reading or sensing someone else's emotions, but Empaths are tuned into these feelings even above those deemed "highly sensitive" on that scale. Being an Empath goes way beyond simply having empathy. Being empathetic simply means your heart goes out to someone that is going through something. Empaths have a greater sense of intuition, creativity, compassion, and even deeper connections to the natural world and other people. Studies have shown that up to 1 in 20 are Empaths-meaning it's much more common that we may have been led to believe. Being an Empath is simply a genetic disposition-it's character trait, and it's just how some of us were made. So how do you know if you've got this disposition?

There are Scientifically validated scales that many types of research have created to accurately and definitively measure empathy. There are various self-tests you can find in print and online that will give you somewhat accurate results as to where you fall on the scale. The best place to start is to get a basic understanding of what empathy really is. We'll dive deeper into the science behind empathy in the next chapter but a basic understanding regarding the difference between simply having empathy for others and actually being an Empath is that having empathy means you are motivated to alleviate the distress of others while being an Empath means you actually feel the distress which creates the need to alleviate it for the both of you.

There are various definitions to describe the many ways that we exhibit or encompass empathy such as Cognitive Empathy, The Theory of the Mind, Empathic Accuracy, Perspective Taking, etc. All of these define the internally knowing the state of another person. Another definition refers to a feeling the same emotion as another known as Emotional Contagion, and emotional/affective empathy. This is referring to having an affective connection with one's emotional state relating to behavioral mimicry. Both imply processing other's emotions and emotional states.

You don't have to be an expert in the theory of the mind to increase your capacities as an Empath. Simply having a basic ability to discern between your own thoughts and emotions, and those that you're picking up from other people or situations is the only requirement. The ability to perceive and respond to others with affective sensitivity is ideal for anyone but it's a commonly known attribute to the Empath. On the other end of that spectrum, the lack of this sensitivity to the distress in others is typically found in those with abnormal neural responses. Think of it as psychopaths lacking basic empathy for others.

Intuitive connections that are automatic and mostly unconscious drive an Empath as they tend to operate by sensing, feeling, and reacting to the most subdued cues. Most Empaths feel they are being called to help and mold our world. Many can perceive spiritual urges, physical sensitivities as well as the understanding what the motivations and intentions of others are. It is thought that Empaths hold an incredible amount of energy and can project that energy outward when releasing or portraying emotions. The Empath can unwittingly access Universal Knowledge and be guided to solve anything they put their heart and mind into. Intuitive Empaths can take this a step further by reflecting on input and give insight into why someone may be feeling the way they are. Not all Empaths have this ability to use their Intuition, though since the many are not able to turn inward and consult the unconscious mind to asses and understand situations.

There are many challenges to the Empath as it's quite easy for them to become over-stimulated as they absorb the emotions and feelings of others. Before realizing they are an

Empath, one could have a lot of stress surrounding normal social situations and could be inclined to unconsciously numb their emotions. Understanding others, connecting to their emotional experiences and infer their thoughts is essential to effectively navigate the social world. Effective social functioning relies on the extent to which one can empathize with others. This is related to prosocial behaviors like cooperation and helping. Prosocial behavior benefits other people directly, or society. This includes sharing, helping, donating, co-operating and volunteering. Our empathy is what shapes the landscape of our lives socially as it motivates this prosocial behavior, facilitates cooperation, inhibits aggression, and motivates our caregiving. Many Empaths are suffocated by intimate relationships, and they tend to not have the same defenses as other people. Empaths even have issues with the fabric of their clothing as certain fabrics such as wool tend to cause great irritation and skin flare-ups. Many Empaths exhibit a low pain threshold-again their hyper-sensitive nature coming into play.

When energy fields overlap, especially in public spaces, Empaths can feel all of them and all that information and energy can be translated into the Empath's body. If one is not able to process this information in a positive, or at least neutral way, it can end up manifesting in their body as Anxieties, and both Depressive and Panic Disorders. Learning how to keep from burnout is a top priority.

There can be both Introverted and Extroverted Empaths

thought it's rarer for an Extroverted Empath since they typically enjoy going out more and socializing. Many Empaths enjoy solitary activities where their creative juices can flow and simply be allowed to happen. In either case, after going out an Empath typically has a great need for decompression. Much of their energy is renewed through deep sleeping. Many that are unable to process as information as it comes in will process these energies during sleep. It can be very beneficial for an Empath to keep a Dream Journal and logging every time they can.

Some Empaths can't handle the solitude to process everything and they rely on other people to help them process what they're going through. Empaths typically need to have some sort of caring, supportive environment available to help them. There needs to be a spirit of inclusion and respect for diversity.

There are many books and even documentaries that have been created that are legitimizing the Empath's experience. Many of these focus on the synchronicities and the experiencing of déjà vu that are common in Empaths and can lead them to an understanding of who they are by identifying and appreciating the connections. Paranormal experiences, near-death experiences, and out-of-body experiences, which are also common for them, can provide momentum to self-discovery.

While many of us feel and express empathy, how do we know when we are a full-blown Empath? Many of us realize that we are a bit different from others at a young age while others seem to never identify why they are so sensitive to the world. Thankfully, there are dozens and dozens of quizzes available online and in books for determining if you are just a highly sensitive person or living as an Empath.

Below are common traits and characteristics found on these quizzes. If you identify with some or all of these, chances are you are beginning your journey into becoming a fully-developed Empath.

- Appearing disconnected, shy, or aloof
- Prone to mood swings and detests pretending to be happy
- Having feelings that are associated with the days of the week. Even when not working a typical work week, they can pick up on a collective feeling
- Drawn to exploring, adventure, travel, and in general, is a free spirit
- Exhibits addictive personalities-mostly as a coping mechanism aiding in blocking of other's emotions
- Chronic Fatigue
- Overeating/Overindulgent behavior to cope with Stress
- Startles easily
- Easily feeling sad when others around are sad
- Easily understanding what makes friends happy
- Becoming upset when someone else is being treated disrespectfully

- Feelings of excitement when someone else is feeling excited
- Concerned and gentle feelings towards people that are less fortunate than you
- Easily able to see things from another person's point of view
- Often "in-tune" with other people's moods
- Taking time to listen to arguments even if you know that you are right
- Making the effort and enjoying making others feel better
- Lower back problems and Digestive Disorders-Issues stemming from the Solar Plexus Chakra
- Being labeled as overly sensitive
- Strong reactions to medications and stimulants
- Self-imposed social isolation
- Feeling replenished by visits to Nature
- Not identifying with others and feeling like your perspective is unique/identifying with everyone
- Feeling compelled to take care of others even when it's detrimental to self
- People refer to you as an "Old Soul"
- Water in all its forms brings you comfort-swimming, bathing, cleansing

Once you've determined that you fall somewhere on the Empathic Spectrum, it is critical that you get the techniques and tools to be able to use hone and use your gifts. It is very easy for a newly discovered Empath to fall prey to depression, disconnection, addictions, and mental exhaustion. The necessary steps to embrace your new-found identity and ability. You are entering a new phase of your life and shifting into a new paradigm where you understand and relate to your true self. Explore your inner and outer workings. Accept yourself and start to reflect your temperament through your actions.

In a world where so many people are cut off from their emotions, being an Empath is comparable to having super powers. This can be your greatest strength.

2

The Biological and Physiological Causes of Being an Empath

W hat is the Science behind Empathy and what makes Empaths brain systems different from anyone else? Breaking down the Science behind what causes a person to be an Empath can be very useful when trying to explain what you're feeling and why you're feeling it. It's also a great way to help identify what type of Empath you are and how you can best use your abilities. What's the difference between a Highly Sensitive Person and an Empath?

It's important to note that not all Empaths are empathetic. Just because one can feel the emotions of someone else doesn't mean that they have accepted that ability, or that they care to use it. That isn't to say that they can't be kind-just simply that they typically don't want to understand or simply do not care about the reciprocal relationship of how their actions affect other human beings. There are also people that are extremely empathetic but are not actually Empaths. Those people would be considered Highly Sensitive People, and while they might not be considered Empaths, all Empaths can be considered Highly Sensitive Persons.

Empathy is like a personality trait as it manifests itself differently in each person. Unfortunately, a lot of the Scientific Community will refer to Empaths as having a "Sensory Processing Disorder." On the flip side-most people in the Metaphysical and Spiritual communities would consider it a gift. A gift that can be managed and appreciated and is meant to be impressed and enhanced, not suppressed. Another issue with the Scientific Community is that there is a tendency to pathologize one's perceptual capacities-which has resulted in some Empaths having been institutionalized. Thankfully, new evidence is surfacing surrounding the current research into the ability showing that Empathy is not just a product of the mind.

This change in perception of empathy in the Scientific community is largely due to research in neurobiology, and brain research. Imaging has been able to demonstrate the existence of our neural relay mechanisms that allow

Empaths to exhibit mimicry of postures, expressions, and mannerisms unconsciously compared to those that are not empathetic. The same motor and sensory areas of an Empaths brain match the person they are observing. This means that the expression "I feel your pain" is literal. There have recently been neuro-imaging studies to find how Empaths feel the pain of others in an attenuated form. This attenuation is key because if we literally felt the same thing as everyone else-it would render us useless.

Once believed to be an inborn trait that could not be taught, research is starting to show that empathy is mutable and can be taught. Scientists have often asked why our brains are designed for this intricate, complex task. If we were wired to simply dominate others as is implied with "survival of the fittest" why are we able and even drawn to respond to our fellow humans suffering? Our capacity to not only perceive but to resonate with other's emotions and feelings allows us to understand and help them. This is because the survival of our species depends on mutual aid- a very powerful force in our world.

In the mid-19th century aestheticism brought forth the concept of empathy. The German "Einfuhlung" describes the "emotional knowing" from within by feeling the emotional resonance. Mostly relating to works of art, the concept was expanded to mean that inner imitation of the actions of others plays a critical role in eliciting empathy.

Simply put, it means being able to feel one's way into the experiences of another. More texture was added to this definition and the empathetic relationship by including the finding that humane respect and concern for another being contrasted with objectifying and dehumanizing others which are found often in our modern societies.

There is a balance between empathy leading us to help or distancing ourselves due to our own distress. We tend to have the most empathy for others that look and act like us. Those that may have suffered in a similar way as us, and those who share a common goal. This means that social and culturally based perceptions can be triggering subconsciously when we feel or empathize with someone else. The way we value someone that is in need either increases or decreases our empathy for them. That is why it's extremely important for cognitive empathy to play a role in healthcare settings. The neuro-autonomy of our brains can allow us to feel empathy for others but can also stop us from making cross-cultural connections. Highly empathic people are more motivated and successful in attending to others' emotional states and will often have the same neural representations activated in themselves.

Because Empathy is a complex capability that enables us to understand and even feel the emotional states of others, it leads to us having compassionate behavior. Being Empathic means that you have the required cognitive, behavioral, emotional, and moral capacities of both the understanding and responding to the suffering and experiences of others. Without empathy, one cannot have compassion as they are interconnected leading from "perception to response" or "observation to action."

Some of the testing and scales created in the scientific community relate to one's cognitive empathy for each of the six basic emotions. Many tests that determine if you are an Empath will essentially assess your capability to connect cognitively and affectively with others experiencing surprise, sadness, happiness, fear, disgust, and/or anger. Each of these basic emotions has subscales to find the extent to which one affectively connects with and feels with that person's specific emotion. There are those working to develop a better understanding of the concept of Empathy and the individual differences of those with this trait.

Let's explore some of the ways empathy can be tested, and the ways it manifests in our bodies on a biological and physiological level.

Empathy Quotient

To measure empathy exclusively, many Scientific assessments focus on the level of social impairment in certain disorders, or Empathy Quotient. Since levels of empathy are different between each person these types of measurements can be used as a casual measure for temperamental empathy. To test ones Empathy Quotient, tests will include around 40 items that relate to empathy and 20 control items.

Some of the questions you would find on an Emotional Quotient Test:

-I dream most nights

-I live for today rather than the future

-people tell me that I'm unpredictable

-I can't always see why someone would be offended by a remark

-I usually stay emotionally detached when watching films

-I am at my best first thing in the morning

By the way you report how likely, or unlikely you are to identify with certain statements, these tests can help determine on a measurable scale where you fall regarding being extremely unempathetic all the way through highly empathetic.

Vicarious States

When we witness the emotional states of others, Empaths tend to replicate them in their selves as if they *were* them. Empaths have a natural ability to mentalize these experiences so vividly that they take prosocial behavioral steps to mitigate the emotion. Prosocial behavior can be explained as conforming to socially accepted behaviors and obeying the rules. It's having the intent to benefit others, and/or society. It's been found that for both empathetic and vicarious emotions are both highly functional in social situations and interactions.

Electromagnetism

In addition to the energy generated by our brains and hearts, this includes the electromagnetic energies of the Earth and of other people and even animals. Empaths can sense these energies and use them to transmit information on both Linear and Spiritual levels. It's been said that the magnetic field produced by our hearts is 100 times greater than what's generated by our brains and can be detected up to 3 feet away from our bodies! For Empaths, this information about someone's emotional state is projected in this energy and communicated into the external environment.

Increased Dopamine Sensitivity

The neurotransmitter Dopamine is associated with our pleasure response. It seems that Empaths need less of the chemical to feel "happy" and are in general, more content with solitude and in need of less external stimulation. This means smaller amounts of Dopamine are being produced with Empaths because it takes less of it to get the desired response. This is a huge benefit for Empaths because many people suffer from low levels of Dopamine, and struggle to maintain a positive outlook in its absence.

Synesthesia

Synesthesia is an extremely common attribute of Empaths. It can be explained as a perceptual phenomenon involving involuntary secondary cognitive pathways being stimulated. This means that one of your senses can be triggered by a completely unrelated sense that was triggered. For example, if someone is Angry, an Empath could interpret, mirror, and respond to the same emotions quite differently. This is because the behavioral consequences of each emotion are different, and the extent that one can empathize with someone varies greatly depending on the emotion expressed. When thinking of Anger, it's typically an emotion caused by experiencing obstacles while in pursuit of a goal leading to a perceived unfairness and a strong desire to fight the obstacle. Empaths, being sensitive, may be likely to experience fear or sadness in response, or if they are attuned to Anger emotions-they could engage in mirrored aggressive behaviors. Another way Synesthesia manifest is by increasing one's willingness to help when connecting with someone experiencing sadness, or loneliness.

Also described as having a "hidden sense" Synesthesia will typically be exhibited in two forms: Projective and Associative.

- Projective Synesthesia- With this form a person will usually see color impressions, forms and/or shapes that relate to the main stimulus. An example would be associating numbers with colors and vice versa.

- Associative Synesthesia- With this form, there is a strong connection to stimulus and the sense that it triggers. Imagine hearing an instrument and very strong feeling or thinking that it sounds like a color. Also known as "colored hearing" Associative

Synesthetes see colors in their mind's eye or have visions near to their body when they hear music, voices, and sounds. Other common forms would include "hearing colors" and "tasting words."

Synesthesia is further broken down into groups that allow us to explore each type further.

- **Grapheme/Color**

This time of Synesthetes typically referred to "color synesthetes" can see different letters and numbers in unique colors. Imagine reading a book where every letter had its own color. Obviously, this can cause a sensory overload leading to exhaustion and burn out in anyone but can be completely overwhelming when the Synesthetic is an Empath.

- **Chromesthesia**

Known for associating sounds to color. When a sound is heard, it is accompanied by color. This happens automatically, and the person doesn't have the ability to assign what color fits each sound.

- **Ordinal-Linguistic Personification**

This uncommon style of Synesthesia occurs when a person associates *things* with the attributes of a person and even animals. An example would be where one may see a number as a person such as 1 being a skinny man or the number 7 is a female celebrity with blonde hair. Also known for assigning personalities and/or genders to ordinal numbers, days, months, and even letters. This form tends to occur alongside those with Grapheme-Color Synesthesia as these personifications are automatically revoked.

- **Number-Form Synesthesia**

Known for the involuntary and automatic forming of a mental map, called a number form, made up of numbers whenever one thinks of numbers. Because numbers are assigned/mapped into distinct spatial locations, it makes it easier to access the information when needed and relate it to a situation. These types are very good at remembering details with numbers such as license plates and telephone numbers.

- **Lexical-Gustatory**

Words are connected to having a taste. The words that trigger a response and the response received greatly varies between synesthetes.

• Misophonic

Considered a neurological disorder, it is related to or even one variety of Synesthesia. These types experience negative feelings triggered by sounds. These feelings typically include annoyance, anger, and disgust. This could be caused by hearing seemingly annoying sounds like slurping or chewing ice, but also normal sounds like typing on a keyboard, talking, and saying certain words repetitively causing a form of sound-emotion synesthesia.

• Auditory-Tactile

Another rare form of Synesthesia, these types experience certain sounds and noises that cause sensations in certain parts of their body. This can be explained as someone hearing a specific word feels touch in a part of their body. It also could mean that sounds to create a sensation in the skin without having been touched.

• Mirror-touch

An intense form where one feels the same physical sensation of another. Those with this type of Synesthesia usually have higher empathy levels than most others. Thought to be related to mirror neurons that have been linked to empathy as well. For example, if one experiencing Mirror-Touch observes someone breaking their finger they may feel extreme pain in their own finger.

It's important to keep in mind that while many Synesthetes are Empaths, not all Empaths are Synesthetes. Most people will have experienced Synesthesia at some point in their lives whether they were conscious of it or not. As babies, we respond to stimulus in this type of way until we've experienced enough to make our own connections over time.

Mirror Neurons

As mentioned as a type of Synesthesia, these neurons are a specialized group of brain cells that are responsible for compassion. They reflect, or "mirror" what goes on in other people so that we can feel it, especially in the ones that we love. This is essentially the reciprocal empathy of "I feel your pain." This doesn't mean that it's always good or beneficial. The discovery of mirror neurons was a huge scientific breakthrough because it means that our brains work not only via the traditional logical interpretations but also through *feeling*. These are the only brain cells we currently know of that are seemingly specialized to code our own actions and the actions of others. This leads us to simulate the emotions and intentions associated with those actions. This is essentially the basis of much of Eastern Philosophy that says we are connected quite literally by your neurons. To understand this visually, imagine the energy coming off your body mixing with the energy coming off someone else. When these energies commingle, they join in a way that makes it hard to discern one from the other. This implies that, in the form of energy, there is no real distinction between your consciousness from someone else's.

True Empaths are thought to have hyper-responsive mirror neurons, allowing them to deeply resonate with other people's feelings. Mirror neurons may provide the biological basis of human self-awareness. As they not only help simulate other people's behavior, they can be turned "inward" creating representations of those earlier brain processes. That means mirror neurons may be responsible for the neural basis of introspection and reciprocity of self and other awareness. There is an entire realm of metaphysical secrets that have been opened by cognitive neuroscientists within the mirror neuron modular brain. The significance of these cells has become increasingly controversial. The question they are now asking is what remains to be learned from them? It's been speculated that Mirror Neurons may run a type of virtual reality simulation of what it would be like for oneself to perform an action (think "walk in shoes"). There are also studies focusing on why some i...dividuals diagnosed with Autism are found to have impairment when it comes to understanding the thoughts and intentions of others, while there are just as many findings showing that some people with Autism have no problem whatsoever understanding the actions of others.

Mirror Neurons are a controversial subject in the scientific community. For those that advocate that mirror neurons play a central role in our ability to understand other people's actions -there is an argument that states we fully understand many things even if we don't have the necessary motor cells or understanding to simulate them. Think of seeing a bird fly. We understand what the bird is doing, and how it is doing it, even where it may be going-even though we couldn't simulate the birds' action with our own motor cells. While it's possible to understand actions without corresponding mirror neuron activity, these neurons seem to bring an extra depth to our understanding. It seems universally recognized that Mirror Neurons play a significant role in important social cognition. While not *making* us empathic, they certainly help us decide *how* we imitate and empathize with each other.

Somatic Empathy

This is a type of physical reaction we experience in the somatic nervous system, thought to be based on mirror neuron responses. This can be useful as by watching and mirroring our peers we are able to connect and feel more comfortable with others. It's also a testament to how fully processed your emotions and feelings are. You are much more likely to experience positive and relaxing reactions if you have worked through any unresolved emotions about a way of being within yourself.

Empathy leads to replenishment and renewal of vital human capacity. Working to enhance our native capabilities to empathize is critical to strengthening our individual, community, national, and international bonds. Empathy plays such a large societal role in providing an emotional bridge as it enables the sharing of experiences, needs, and desires. Even if you're not an Empath, there are many steps you can take to increase your inherent ability to empathize with others and make a significant, positive change in the world.

3

What Are Empaths Sensitive to?

E mpaths have a wide array of sensitivities and you can potentially identify solely as one type or with multiple types. You'll begin to learn yourself more and identify what talents you have that can work for the good of yourself and others. Since taking on the emotions of others is common in all Empaths, you'll want to be prepared for sudden and potentially overwhelming emotions when you are in public. Remember that even though a vibe from a person or space can cause undesirable feelings, there are many places of beauty that can be transformative for Empaths.

As an Empath, you will need to find ways of coping with the increased sensitivity you have to basic senses such as taste, touch, smell, light, sound, and temperature. Many Empaths are very sensitive to bright lights, and loud noises. When these are encountered unexpectedly it can be quite jarring and may send a shock to your body. You might find that you startle much easier than others because of that heightened sensitivity to sensory input. This includes strong smells and chemicals such as foods, perfumes, chemicals, etc. You can feel physically ill when you encounter everyday aromas that seemingly go unnoticed by others.

As an Empath, your body can be depleted or energized by intense weather. This can vary greatly from one person to another-where one may feel completely drained from experiencing a thunderstorm, another could feel replenished. The same goes for clear, sunshine days, full moons, snow, etc.

Your sensitivities can become overloaded just by exposing yourself to certain people and/or situations. When you add additional symptoms such as being sick, dealing with grief and loss, or the regular stress of work and family it can rapidly deteriorate your quality of life.

On your journey, you may find that you have sensitivities when it comes to certain people, objects, places, or situations. It can help to identify all the elements that you are sensitive to when you are exploring your ability to attune to the energies and control them. Below are some of the more common types of empathic sensitivities or types.

Empath Sensitivity Types

- **ANIMAL/ FANNA-** Ability to tune into animals and even communicate with them. Can you feel what an animal needs? Does it seem that animals are simply drawn to you? Do you prefer the company of animals even over other people at times? Careers involving animal healing, biology, or psychology can be extremely fulfilling and rewarding for Empaths of this type.

- **EARTH or GEOMANTIC-** Includes the earth, solar system, and even weather. An innate knowledge of the past, current, and future states of any region. Are you able to read energy and signals seemingly coming directly from the earth? May feel the energies of impending natural disasters. Do you feel attuned to your physical landscape? Are you drawn to sacred places such as cemeteries, churches, groves? You could have a sensitivity to the history of a place and be able to pick up on emotions that occurred in those locations. Do you grieve for damage caused to our natural world? These types can feel rested and recharged by simply spending time secluded in nature. Helping with environmental projects can be very healing for these types. Surrounding yourself with natural objects and plants in your living space as well as natural linens and body care products can help you feel balanced and cared for.

- **ENVIRONMENTAL**- Empaths of this type are highly attuned to any changes that have happened or may occur in a physical space. Have you entered a room or space and just known things that have happened there? Have you held or touched objects and understood information about their owner? This sensitivity can extend out to the plants and animals that inhabit a particular space.

- **PSYCHOMETRIC-** These Empaths possess the ability to *read* physical objects. Are you able to feel energies from photographs, other people's jewelry, etc.? They can typically hold an item of interest and be able to understand the energies of those that have encountered it, or the energies of the place it resides, etc.

- **PLANT/FLORA**- connect with the essence and needs of plants. Do you feel drawn to nature? Do you have a green thumb though no one else in your family or circle has one? You may intuitively understand how to care and tend to all types of plants. Do you innately know what plants uses and functions are? Do you feel drawn to ecological balance and have an interest in sustainability? Plants will thrive in your presence and it nurtures your strong connection to what plants and trees offer us and need from us.

- **MEDIUMSHIP**- The ability to access spirits on the Other Side. Having these sensitivities allow an Empath to communicate with the Astral and other planes as easily as they communication on this plane. They must work to shut off their minds when they are not in the position to be receptive as they are always prone to intrusion from spirits and energies.

- **INTELLECTUAL-** Ability to communicate with many forms of vocabulary and jargon. Empaths with this type of sensitivity may find it easy to adapt their communication styles and adapt to whoever they may be speaking with. Most times this mirroring happens unconsciously.

- **INTUITIVE-** includes Psychic, Telepathic, Precognitive, and Dream Empaths. Ability to experience extraordinary perceptions including intuition and telepathy. Do you have an innate sense of just complete understanding or knowing? Can you tell when people are lying? Are you able to see someone's intentions for what they really are? Also known as **spiritual** or **claircognizant empaths**, you may have a direct connection to other realms. Can you feel physical or emotional symptoms from communications with the spiritual world? In Eastern philosophy, it is known as Enlightenment. Those things such as metaphysics and the quantum world that can be beyond the average human intellect can be accessed and comprehended easily by Empaths of this type. This

Intuitive Sensitivity can manifest itself in one or all the following distinctions:

- Psychic- receive energies and information about and from others in the present time
- Precognitive- Premonitions about your or other's futures in both waking and dream states
- Dream- receives energies and information through dreams to help and guide self and others

- **EMOTIONAL/ AFFECTIVE-** Ability to pick up **and respond to** other's emotions-essentially a sponge for others feelings-negative or positive. Do you just know when someone is depressed or sad, or happy without speaking with them? Do you see through any façade someone may be putting up to mask how they truly feel?

- **PHYSICAL**- Can absorb physical symptoms and reflect the emotions or feelings of other persons. Do you have an innate ability to sense what someone needs regarding healing? Do you get headaches out of the blue when you know someone near you is suffering from one? This can be true for energies as well- when you are around someone with negative or low levels of energy, yours may drop as well. The same is true for positive energies. Since the pain someone else feels can manifest in your body-it can be extremely useful when you are healing.

- **HEYOKA**- Native American Term- the person that functions as a trickster, disrupter, or a go-between. Empathic ability to move between this physical world and the Spiritual worlds. Psychic mediums and communicators. They absorb others emotions and feelings and can act as a mirror to show people what they may need to see about themselves or what they need to change.

Take the time to explore how you react to each of the types. Put yourself in situations that will bring out your abilities so that you can confirm if you have any sensitivities there. For further introspection, you may want to consider the impact that Astrological signs have on the types of empathic sensitivities we are predisposed for. These correlate with your natural personality traits and can influence the type of Empathic Abilities you will want to focus on developing.

The twelve signs of the zodiac fall under the elements of fire, air, water, and earth. Each element has three signs. Water signs are typically highly emotional and are sensitive to psychic energies. These signs, Scorpio, Pisces, and Scorpio all tend to have empathic abilities and it's common for them to be highly sensitive Empaths. If you are familiar with Astrology and the Zodiac, you may be familiar with what sign of the zodiac that the Sun was in at the time of your birth. Understand that knowing your Sun sign can give you insight into your life force energies, self-expression, and it can represent a key part of your identity. Also knowing your Moon Sign and your Rising Sun will give you a deeper picture of who you are and help you to dive deeper into what sensitivities you are more in tune with.

Zodiac Indications

Aries -The Ram – Fauna Empaths

Known for initiating or harnessing the force of Spring. Typically, those in the Aries sign will be close to animals and can connect with them better than others. This can manifest in hunting or fishing as well as they are drawn to be an integral part of the circle of life. They are also known as the trailblazer of the signs. Aries energy helps us to fight for beliefs and put ourselves out there.

Taurus -The Bull – Physically Receptive Empath

Those under the sign of Taurus will experience strong feelings that are manifested in the physical world. They are known for mirroring the emotions of others into their own bodies, even experiencing psychosomatic symptoms. As the provider in the zodiac, the Taurus energy helps us get the job done, and seek security.

Gemini – The Twins – Telepathic Empath

Extremely sensitive people that can attune to voices and vibes from everyone around them. They can enhance this ability to send and receive messages to anyone. Gemini energy helps us with our ability to connect and communicate with others. Known for being vibrant and one of the most versatile, Geminis can learn to maintain an open mind, and use power responsibly.

Cancer – The Twins – Chameleon Empath

A natural nurturer, and the most sensitive and purest type of Empath. They have a natural ability to feel emotions and are changed by it. Their psyche can change like the water in tides, and they can see the bigger picture allowing them to course correct. Those born under this sign are almost always highly sensitive people and as a Water Sign, are usually Empaths. Selenite can help protect Cancers from negative energies.

Leo – The Lion- Psychometric Empath

Leo energy guides us to express ourselves and wear our heart on our sleeves. Psychometric Empaths can feel vibes just by touching something someone else once held. By spending time with an object, they allow it to gradually affect their mood. They must take care as sometimes they can't shake the feeling off.

Virgo- The Virgin-Flora Empath

Naturally, in tune with the needs of others, Virgos can also be affected or affect flowers, plants, trees, and the natural environment in a supernatural way. As botanicals are closely related to our psyche's, Virgos can hone their skills by immersing themselves in the natural world and cultivating healing herbs. Known for being able to attune to the forces of plants and trees, they can pick up on energies of the natural world. Virgo energy helps us to prioritize the well-being of ourselves, those around us, and the planet.

Libra- The Scales - Emotionally Receptive Empath

Those under this sign seem to be genuinely indecisive as they take time to weigh everyone's emotions. Filtering through these emotions can make those naturally receptive to take control and harness them, increasing their personal power. Libra energy inspires us to seek harmony and coop-eration as well as doing so gracefully.

Scorpio- The Scorpion-Medium Empath

Scorpio energy is extremely focused and intense. These types are naturally able to sense spirits and invisible entities and can make for the best conjurers. While helping us to dive deep and form indestructible bonds, they rely on having beacons of lights from others. This sign can be the most intense, and they need to feel safe and secure. If they don't have this safe environment, their connection with the spiritual realm will be hidden due to judgment from others. As another Water Element, they are typically Empaths that seek guidance and advice from spirits. Smoky Quartz can help protect them from bad vibes.

Sagittarius- The Archer -Enlightened Empath

The Adventurer of the Zodiac, Sagittarius seems to always look for the meaning to life and can empathically sense truth inside others. This energy encourages us to seek the truth of the world and take fearless risks. They can function as a walking lie detector able to see through any façade and view someone's real intentions.

Capricorn- The Goat-Geomantic Empath

Capricorn energy leads us towards the power of structure and a measured master plan. They seem to be able to sense what's troubling mother nature through geomantic waves.

This zodiac sign tends to know instantly if something is right or wrong with a place.

Aquarius- The Water Bearer-Gaia Empath

These signs empathic ability is very powerful because of their ability to connect to everything and everyone around them. They can also sense the areas around them like a Geomantic Empath and will usually feel out regions and even continents by deliberately scanning areas. This sign typically holds the highest level of earthly empathy. This energy pulls us to unite for social justice and innovation.

Pisces- The Fish -Astral Empath

Known for being the dreamers and natural healers of the zodiac, Pisces can also sense what's happening in different planes. With practice they can reach the Astral Plane, helping others to realize emotions before they experience them. Pisces energy draws us towards compassion here on the Material Plane. Amethyst can help protect those under this water sign from negative energies.

Use this information to develop into the person you are meant to be. Letting yourself be the person that you are meant to become is the best thing you can do when living as an Empath. Take care to not only prevent the unwanted energies and emotions of others to permeate your aware-ness, work to keep yourself from projecting your vibration onto others. It doesn't matter where you are starting from, it only matters that you're moving in the right direction. Notice the vibrational energy that you are emitting and understand that *you* are the dominant element in your life and what you manifest.

Vibration and Resonating with Energetic Fields

Most Empaths have a strange ability to cause disruptions and reactions with electrical currents. Have you experienced strange glitches, drained batteries though you just charged a device, flashing lights, and scrambled messages? If so, you are probably experiencing the phenomena associated with Empaths and Energies. The human body has the capability to send and receive energy to and from its environment and other people. This exchange of energy can also influence our thoughts and emotions. This can happen when we are near each other and is heightened with actual touch. Touching will cause our brains to produce biochemical responses but our electromagnetic fields intersecting can make one feel as if you are aligning energetically. Typically, these types of interactions from our heart fields go on beneath our level of awareness, but for Empaths, this magnetic attraction and repulsion happen with not only notice but with clarity.

You may have encountered something that tells you to

"raise your vibration." If you have ever wondered what that really means or wanted to know how you do that you should start with understanding attraction and resonance. Think of it as your emotions vibrating in your chakras, and aura. The beliefs you have and your experiences will make up the way you perceive reality. When you are focusing on low vibration emotions such as shame, or guilt, you are resonating that energy or vibration. These emotions generate responses such as humiliation, destruction, and blame. The energy and vibration that you are putting out there will continually attract other people, experiences, and situations that resonate with those vibrations. On the opposite end of the emotional vibrational spectrum, the highest on the scale would be feelings of joy, love, peace, and enlightenment. These will generate responses such as revelation, insight, serenity, and even bliss.

Manipulating Vibrations

So *how* do we raise our personal vibrations? First, consider anything that you carry with you that is not your vibration. Think about how what you are carrying attracts what you do not want. When we are conscious of our intention, we can evolve our awareness and assimilate these experiences to clear our energy fields. When we do this, new opportunities will automatically generate as well as experiences and connections. Work on getting those low vibrations out of your field. This will get you more in tune with your authentic self.

As your energetic vibration raises and resonates, you will have access to higher levels of consciousness. Practice stabilizing your hold on higher vibrational resonance, it can change everything for you. When you feel there is an imbalance, or if you think you could benefit from healing energy, you may want to contact a practitioner of energy healing. There are many forms of "energy medicine" that you can practice including magnet therapy, color puncture, and light therapy. You can find practitioners if the fields of Reiki, Qigong, distance healing, therapeutic touch, contact healing, spiritual healing, and bio field energy healing. It's thought that these healers act as a channel that can pass a type of bio-electromagnetism. These types of harmonic resonance healing are meant to be more in depth and provide you with ongoing healing.

There are ways to easily raise your vibration on your own. Give someone a hug, organize your work or living space, surround yourself with people you know raise you up, listen to music you love, breathe deeply, eat raw foods, etc. Understanding the energy, you carry with you and naturally create will help you interpret the sensitivities you'd like to develop and attune to.

. . .

Aura

You may be familiar with the human energy field that surrounds our bodies. This energy field is made up of bands of energy we call auric layers or fields. They encompass our bodies and connect us to the outside world. Thought to share properties with the electromagnetic field, it's composed of opposites or polarities. In this auric field, however, like attracts like. Many Empaths have a permeable aura which is why taking on the energy of others can be debilitating. Working on that mind-body-spirit balance can help deflect the energies of others from entering your aura.

Schedule an Aura Reading. In-depth information about your empathic gifts are encoded in your aura, and it can be both liberating and enlightening to have someone go over this with you. Use that information to start picking up on the auras of your loved ones and people you work with. You can use your senses to see an aura and using your intuition will help. Once you have a good understanding of your own aura you can allow yourself to feel and see the auras of others. You will typically see a color associated with an Aura.

There are many ways to interpret the colors, but it can be

helpful to understand a few basic qualities or keywords of the most common aura colors:

Blue- Calm, balanced, and have an eased nervous system

Turquoise- Multitasker, highly energized, Influencer

Pink- Neutral Energy, Rare, Material/Spiritual Balance

Green- Restful, Healing, Comfort.

White- Mismatched harmony, healing, Innocent

Red- Materialistic, Passion, High Energy Low Frequency

Purple- Psychic/Spiritual ability, Sensitive

Yellow-Inspiration, Freedom, Generosity, High level of Spiritual development

Brown, Gray, muddled Colors- Negative Energies, anger, disease

Just like you can clear your chakras, you can clean your aura. Emotional issues and spiritual problems can throw your aura "out of sync." Imbalances can leave you feeling disconnected and negative. Start with visualizing your aura and concentrate on your breath. Visualize a light encompassing you and spreading far and wide. This simple technique can realign your energies and cleanse the energy built up in your aura. You can maintain it by keeping yourself healthy, not dwelling on negative thoughts, smudging with safe or ceremonial herbs, and commit to kindness. These will all brighten your aura and moods and will improve the relationships you have with yourself and others.

Remember that the Earth is a living being. Connecting to the Earth's resonance is crucial to our well-being and even more important for Empaths. We will move more comfortably through this world if we can focus on adjusting our energetic bodies and nervous systems. Our internal shifts begin with our bodies. We enjoy being alive through these bodies and being on the Earth right now. We can channel some of this vibration coming from Earth to accelerate our individual growth.

Now that you are aware of the different types of Empaths you can begin to identify where your abilities lie, and what characteristics you'd like to develop in yourself. Self-identifying and working on yourself will help you to increase your sensitivities and use them for the better good.

4

How Empathy Affects Your Daily Life

Having an increased sensitivity to light, sounds, emotions, and energy of other people and animals is essentially a part of every Empath's life. However, living in a high state of sensitivity comes with its challenges. It can be very easy to become overwhelmed, exhausted, and over-stimulated. This can leave Empaths with a vulnerability to depression, anxiety, burnout, and addictions. Of course, there are benefits as well. That deeper connection with others, a highly tuned sense of intuition and creativity, as well as being able to deeply feel and use true compassion.

It's been said that with Empathy, we can think it, feel it, and/or be moved by it. The extent to which you respond to this empathy is also the amount it affects your life. We can learn to regulate our empathy just like we do with other emotions and transform it, especially when in excess, into less stressful states of being, such as compassion. Also known as psych somatization, it's the physical manifestation of mental distress. When we work on developing our skills of empathy and focus on maintaining positive attitudes towards ourselves and others, it can lead to experiencing less negative emotion. Allowing positive experiences to dominate will lend to a healthier state of mind.

Empathy can affect your daily life in the way that you cope with all the ups and downs. Because focusing on the threat is our natural response to stress, an Empath can easily focus on an entire situation including its meaning and implication and the experiences of others. Because you aren't focused on just the threat, you have a wider range of solutions based on the extensive, comprehensive perspective. This, added to the fact that Empaths are drawn to reduce the suffering of others can make us more flexible, understanding, and even kinder. This can lead to the formation of long-lasting compassionate bonds with our close friends and family.

There are struggles that you'll want to watch out for in your everyday life.

Television- We must be mindful of what we allow around us. Watching television or movies can be a great way to unwind or unplug from the day, but while entertaining, many programs will be full of tragedy, violence, and even cruelty. This can emotionally drain an Empath quickly.

Small changes such as, not watching the news at night can go a long way when creating a safe space for yourself mentally.

Saying No- Because we are more naturally inclined to the satisfaction and happiness of others, it can be difficult to say no. We must understand that it's okay to set boundaries and expect others to respect them, and to realize that it will not necessarily cause that person to experience negative feelings.

Getting Out- It's easy to become overwhelmed and intimidated by public places. When you are first realizing that you are an Empath, you find it extremely uncomfortable to be in large social gatherings and that you are completely drained within just a few minutes. Work on strengthening your abilities and shielding yourself from others so that you can enjoy the companionship and experiences out there.

Quiet Time- Take the time you need to recoup from over-stimulation. Work on your own energies and emotions in solitude. You will need to carve out time for yourself every day to focus inward. This can also mean that you need to sleep alone. If you find that you are not getting real rest because you are soaking up the energy and emotion of your significant other, be sure to create personal space for you to sleep.

Fatigue- You probably are already dealing with feeling drained of energy daily. Because of the constant reception you get, it's easy to be worn out and never really feeling entirely rested. You may have been labeled as lazy though you could be the exact opposite. Take care to rest and rejuvenate yourself through quiet time, holidays, and surrounding yourself with peaceful and serene situations. Chronic fatigue can manifest itself into lifelong illness.

Being Empathic can cause you to seek out ways that to numb yourself for the constant bombardment you receive, including things that distract your attention, make you feel disconnected or detached, and sometimes it can cause you to fully isolate yourself away from everyone else. Some of these methods we use to hide can become lifelong problems that we will have to overcome before we can really get in tune with our empathic sensitivities. We'll explore how suppressing the empathic abilities can negatively impact our lives further in Chapter 6.

When we are not in balance or alignment with the natural world around us and our empathic abilities, it can manifest in not only our emotional and spiritual health but our physical lives as well. Because we can shift our vibrations to be higher or lower with substances such as caffeine, alcohol, or drugs, we can easily develop addictions. Turning to drugs and alcohol is common for Empaths looking to ease their edginess. While they provide temporary relief, they will take a toll on them over time physically, emotionally, and spiritually.

. . .

Addiction

In our brains, the neurotransmitter Dopamine is responsible for all pleasure. Since Empaths are born with hypersensitive nervous systems this "reward-related" learning can be easily altered. This can mean that the signals for *liking* something get confused with *wanting* or *needing* it. This means that in addition to the abuse of substances because of the ability to take one out of "empath mode", Empaths can be even more prone to addictions because of this feel-good hormone. Addictive behavior isn't limited to drugs and alcohol. Addictions can present themselves in various ways:

- Drama- Some Empaths find themselves addicted to the Drama they find themselves involved in when experiencing and interacting with the energetic fields of others. This can be abused to drown out emotionally overwhelming situations with drama as a form of redirecting energy.

- Isolation- While it's okay and even recommended that you make time for yourself away from the stresses of the world, you must be careful not to become a recluse-hiding yourself away to avoid people and/or situations. Self-imposed isolation leads to other addictions and increases the potential for depressive moods and other disorders.

- Over-Exercising- Also manifests itself as Over-committing yourself to activities to focus your attention on something other than the way you feel, or the energies of others. This can make a great distraction but when it's an addiction it can be taken to the extremes where there is an increased chance of injury and other physical/mental issues because of the excessive behavior.

- Over Eating/Aggressive Dieting- This includes turning to food to feel better. Certain foods are highly addictive because of the feel-good chemicals they trigger in our bodies or overindulging as over-eating or excessive calorie counting/dieting.

- Compulsive Disorders- Mostly recognized as Obsessive-Compulsive Disorder, this can manifest as obsessive, uncontrollable, reoccurring thoughts. The behaviors can manifest as having the urge to repeat an action repeatedly and even associating rewards and consequences to the completion of that action.

There are always healthy ways to cope with the stress of daily life. Remember that instead of blocking you can surrender. Instead of simply numbing yourself, practice being open. Use the ability you have as an Empath to try a different approach and open yourself up to what you experience. When you do this deliberately, it can change your entire experience.

Beware of cultivating Apathy. By depriving yourself of the small joys that make life worth living, you run the risk of shutting down your empathic abilities. Becoming apathetic will increase your isolation and avoidance not only of activities and people that you used to enjoy but can affect your general levels of interest for life.

When Empaths absorb negative or low-vibration emotions it can impact their vitality, mental state, and essentially their quality of life. These negative emotions can lead to a toxic build-up - having negative implications on physical, emotional, and mental health. Looking for ways to cope with these overwhelming emotions can lead to disaster. Developing healthy coping mechanisms will be crucial for any Empath.

Empathy will not only affect you personally, but it will also have huge impacts on all your relationships, and your career.

. . .

Relationships

When evaluating the relationships, you have with friends, loved ones, colleagues, and even strangers, it's important to distinguish what's working for you and what's not. We *all* have baggage, but you must be able to sort through your own emotional baggage and manage it. This means that you are not taking on others' baggage as well. By taking on the emotional weight that someone else carries, it can lead to that person using it as an excuse for how they treat you and even how they allow you to treat them.

You cannot set someone else's boundaries for them and people that don't recognize or respect your boundaries can compromise your standings or wellbeing. If a significant other that is dealing with their own mental health issues aren't getting the professional help they need, they may not be able to control their impulses and could end up dumping everything on you. It's very easy for these situations to take a negative emotional toll, and lead to an Empath becoming broken. Getting involved with someone that is not able to process and handle their emotions and feelings on their own will very easily expect you to carry them.

You must understand that as an Empath, there are people in the world that *need* the ability you have. There are also people that can hate and despise your ability because you will be a bright light that can shine down on people's brokenness-therefore exposing them. You may be labeled as judgmental. Take care to create personal boundaries and learn how to communicate with others.

Seek out meaningful relationships. There are Empaths that have spent much of their lives single. To some, just the thought of too much togetherness is overwhelming due to the potential amount of sensory overload. It can take quite a while to adjust to intimate relationships for the long-term. Because Empaths rely on their quiet time to replenish themselves, those in relationships must make time to practice self-care.

Being completely honest about your energetic and emotional needs is critical for Empaths in relationships. When your partner understands and respects your sensitivities, you will feel more open and it can really help the intimacy you share with each other. The partner of an Empath should understand that you will need to have alone time daily to keep you sane and happy. You may need to sleep alone or have an area where your rest will be uninterrupted. Compromises will need to be made when it comes to the needs of both of you. Remember that all relationships are a work in progress.

Intimate relationships can be a Spiritual Path as they are about not only companionship but bonding, passion, and the weaving of destinies. Intimate relationships can be unchartered territory, but they can be a magnificent and much-needed journey of discovery. When an Empath truly opens their heart, it can blow others away! Their love can be messy and sometimes hard because of how intense and powerful it can be. Be clear with your partner that this is something about you that you cannot change. It's okay to reject new relationships until you are ready to put in the work and attention it will require.

Career

Many Empaths enjoy successful careers as Writers, Artists, Musicians, Counselors, Healthcare professionals, and even Actors. Typically, the best careers for Empaths are those where they can express their intuition, thoughtfulness, quietness, and creativity. Jobs that require an Empath to behave like someone they are not will be too stifling and stressful. Many Empaths will seek out remote jobs-anything where they can work from home, away from the noise, and energy of a traditional office. Jobs, where one can create their own schedule and take regular breaks will work much better than those with a rigid structure. One must be careful if they do work from home to not over-isolate themselves.

Some of the careers Empaths might seek would include graphic designers, virtual assistants, independent trade workers such as electricians and plumbers that can set their own appointments. Landscape design or other outdoor careers that place you out in nature can be extremely rewarding for Empaths.

Of course, many Empaths will end up working in helping

professions such as doctors, nurses, social workers, teachers, therapists, massage therapists, clergy, and even volunteering for non-profit organizations. Working with animals in all the various forms including veterinary medicine, rescue, and grooming are typical trades for Empaths as well. One must be careful not to take on the stress and symptoms of their clients. Daily meditation and frequent breaks will be just as important as the working schedule.

Professions that are high in physical and emotional trauma or ones that have a large amount of sensory stimulation may prove to be too much for an Empath. Police, Fire-fighters, Emergency medical teams, and even Military jobs can have negative impacts on an Empaths life. Sales and jobs where you constantly deal with the public can take too harsh of a toll on one. This includes cashiering at loud stores-which can quickly exhaust an Empath as they feel that they will have to "be on" for their entire day. Politics, high-level exec-utives, and those in public relations must have the ability to engage in sometimes uncomfortable discussions with many people.

However, even in less than ideal job situations Empaths can typically improvise to create solutions that make the situa-tion more comfortable. They can make important contribu-tions when happy and flourishing at work. Just as anyone needs to take the time to find the type of work that supports their skills, gifts, and temperaments. Being an Empath, you may need to take this a step farther to find a better match by using your intuition to sense if you are a good fit to the shared mission and goals of a company or organization.

As an Empath, you will have to deal with things immediately and learn to give what you get. Remember to keep your guard up. It's easy to lower your guard so that you can be vulnerable and communicate honestly with others. Be sure that you are keeping pace with the people you are dealing with. Don't open yourself too widely as you will be prone and exposed to being overwhelmed.

You will need to create boundaries for what you will accept and won't accept in terms of what you will be around. You may tend to say yes to things even when you do not want to do them or even if it's inconvenient. You can easily be taken advantage of if you are not able to stand up and say No.

Don't hold others to your own ability. Never assume that just because you can understand feelings doesn't mean that others can. There will be others you deal with that have no clue with how they are making you feel. This is common with narcissists, and you must be able to create healthy boundaries. It's easy to have our feelings hurt by others that simply do not understand or care how they make others feel. Don't take the actions of others personally just because you experience them.

Remember that while living as an Empath your day to day life isn't just about fighting overwhelming negative emotions. There is a beautiful side to being an Empath as well. You will absorb compassion, love, and joy. You will feel the excitement of others and allow their emotions of pride and hope fill you as well. You will absorb the love they feel for others, and their kindness. It's these positive emotions that will help you feel balanced, and you should always find ways to surround yourself and immerse yourself in social situations where you will experience these positive emotions.

5

Living as an Empath

C ommon signs an Empath may see in themselves is being highly sensitive to external information and having generous hearts. They are quick to respond to others' needs and can sometimes give too much to others. As an Empath, you will be drawn to certain people, social situations, behaviors, and methods for using your abilities.

Identifying and beginning to utilize the things and spaces you need to thrive should be a top priority for anyone beginning their journey as an Empath. You must realize that being an Empath isn't going to always be glamorous. This is a huge responsibility and it will require a lot of self-control. You'll want to recognize the tendencies you have towards undesirable behaviors. This can include codependency, altruism, and narcissism.

Co-Dependency

This may be the first thing to look for on your journey. In order to serve at your full capacity, you must heal yourself so that you can share your journey. It can be easy to arrive at a point where you care too deeply for someone that creates unhealthy situations. Empaths are used to ensuring those around them are cared for and happy. This can eventually lead many Empaths to turn into co-dependents. If you find yourself rationalizing the actions of someone, or seeking out friends with much larger problems, you may need to take a deeper look at yourself as an Empath.

One of the main characteristics of someone with co-dependency is thinking that constantly worrying about someone is a sign of love. They are always looking for ways to save someone. They run the risk of not ever really knowing who they are because they are constantly busy trying to help people and aren't sure what their actual thoughts are. Trying to please everyone all the time leads to a loss of sense of self. We must understand that in order to love others, we must love ourselves first.

If you realize that you've been exhibiting co-dependent behaviors, you can work on releasing this aspect of yourself. Create a section of your journal dedicated to your thoughts and feelings associated with co-dependency. This can start as recognizing what feelings are their own, and which aren't.

- Take note of how others act in relationships. What emotions are you experiencing from these other people? What emotions are your own?
- Build self-esteem. Recognize your strengths and change the way you think of yourself. Write down something about yourself that's positive every day. Create a space for yourself of self-improvement and forgiveness. Surround yourself with positivity and do things that you enjoy doing.
- Live your own life. Learn what you love and what makes you feel rejuvenated. Create an identity for yourself that is not reliant on any information from others. Make up your own mind. It can take time so be patient with yourself and put in the effort to trusting yourself.
- Practice detaching from others entirely. Give up control over the situations in other people's lives. Relinquish any control or manipulation you have been using.
- Beware of blame and guilt appearing as you heal yourself. These could come from you or from someone you are in a co-dependent relationship with. Understand that everything is not your fault and taking responsibility is only necessary for your own actions.

- Check your Motives. What do you want and need? How are you feeling about it? Just because you care and love for people does not make you co-dependent. If you serve yourself before others and continually check in you will make continual progress.

As an Empath, you are meant to guide others, not control what they do. Their choices are not your fault. You cannot blame yourself for the consequences of their actions. Separating yourself from any codependent behaviors you've had will get you back into alignment and able to use your Empathic ability to truly understand and help others.

Altruism

As related to empathy, it's acting out of concern for someone else. Altruism in its true form will happen regardless of the consequences to self. There are theories surrounding the possibility that people only will act when the reward of it is greater than the cost, and others saying the action is only taken because of the pleasure ones finds when another person experiences relief. These theories prove that one can be inclined to altruistic behavior even when they may not feel empathy. Regardless of the motivations, Scientists have found a neural link between empathy and altruism meaning that if you are an Empath you are highly likely to be sensitive to a stranger's fear and pain.

Unconditional assistance of others, Altruism means that you relieve suffering without any expectation. There is no personal gain or reciprocity to these actions. It can be the antidote to burnout and overstimulation for Empaths. That doesn't mean that all the good deeds people perform are examples of altruism. The act must be completely selfless.

Typically, not part of any social norms, most truly altruistic acts happens when we are in a bad mood. This is because altruistic behavior effectively boosts our moods. Too much of this can be a negative thing, an example of this would be animal hoarding where the person believes they are providing a better environment when they could be causing more harm than good.

On the opposite end of this spectrum of someone exhibiting altruistic behavior, you may find the Narcissist.

Recognizing Narcissism

Empaths must be cautious of the narcissists in life. They tend to only do things for others when they can promote themselves. This can include someone acting as if they are a supporter or protector of certain people until their expectations are missed. They then turn to dismiss those same people and actively working against them. Narcissists also will have you believe that their giving is about you when it's about feeding their fragile egos.

One common characteristic of a narcissist is asking personal questions and offering their guidance. When pushed to provide them with information, they learn as much as they can about you so that they can later claim credit for guiding you or helping you with your accomplishments and goals.

Entitlement is at the core of any narcissist. If they want something, they feel entitled to it-whether that's a physical object or personal attention or admiration.

You may notice that you seem to attract these narcissists like a moth to a flame. By nature, the Empaths purpose in life is healing others and supporting them. Narcissists tend to hide behind their created self-image and seek out Empaths as someone to dump all their baggage on.

Vulnerable Narcissists - These types need to feel special about themselves. They use shaming, gas lighting, and other forms of emotional manipulation to get sympathy and attention from others. Often dealing with inferiority complexes they sometimes merge their identity with those they idealize. Typically, there is a weak inner core to these people that they fear being exposed.

Invulnerable Narcissists - Highly self-confident, and unempathetic they are the traditional image that you think of when considering narcissists. Seeking out recognition and power they have a belief that they are far superior. Unlike vulnerable narcissists, this type truly does believe in their own greatness and can be almost as good as they believe they are.

Subtypes

- **Amorous**- Measure self-worth by sexual conquests. They use their charm along with gifts and flattery to attract someone and then quickly get rid of them as soon as they are deemed boring or their needs have been met. Con artists of relationships they are only out to have their own needs met.
- **Compensatory**- Known for creating illusions of their achievements and of themselves. Seeks out the emotionally vulnerable to act as their audience. They are also known for being extremely sensitive to any criticism. Empaths should be wary of emotional abuse and manipulation that this type uses as their main methods of control.
- **Elitist**-These types will do anything necessary to get to the top and dominate others. Their Ego is inflated, and they have a sense of entitlement that includes their work and family environments. They must always feel intellectually superior and will use their backgrounds and achievements to paint that story.
- **Malignant**- Usually living with personality disorders or diagnosed with psychopathic behavior, this type typically will feel no remorse for their

actions. Feeling that they easily outsmart others, they revel in knowing when they've done so.

- **Covert**- These narcissists will claim that they are Altruistic, or Empathic. This is so that they can claim superiority when it comes to psychic, spiritual, and interpersonal endeavors. This can be found in spiritual and religious communities where they project a positive persona yet use it as a shield that protects them from being held accountable.

Learning to successfully deal with narcissists is essential for Empaths. Start by determining the type you are dealing with. Keep in mind that there are situations that bring out insecurities in people and that you must take note of the context. Being able to deal with narcissists can be done by consistently setting boundaries. If you suspect someone of being a narcissist, try showing dissidence to these people publicly. If they are defensive yet consider what they did incorrectly, you know that they can use their energy to change their perspective and that you can have positive interactions with them. If they attempt to force you to agree, or feel that you should apologize for not agreeing, you may be dealing with a narcissist.

While dealing with these types of people, understand that they may never really like you or become your friend. Many will engage with others simply to increase their network and potential to use them later. Try and hold back criticizing them. You can inflict injury to them and set them off. An effective way to deal with them is to explain that you need their help when you need something from them. Don't ignore them. You may have to work with them and simply acknowledging them and/or their contributions can go a long way.

Though it may be difficult, try and have compassion for them. Understand that underneath the power and intimidation they may exude, there is typically a very fragile person. This doesn't mean that you should attempt to be friends or maintain relationships with them. If you treat them as someone that deals with chronic pain, you can learn to distance yourself from them emotionally and let them be on their way.

Now that you will be living with your newfound knowledge that you are an Empath, you may feel pulled to help other people. There are many aliases that an Empath may be given-Healer, Indigo child/parent, Holistic Practitioner, Lightworker, etc. For example, some of the common signs of being an Indigo person are quite like those of an Empath. Both are on a mission of sorts to both challenge and shift reality. That mission could simply be paving the way for our future generations to create greater peace and harmony for us all. Most of these aliases share the ability to notice, identify, and react to the subtle unspoken thoughts and emotions of others

. . .

Light Working

The main objective of a light worker is aiming to raise everyone's consciousness. These people having a calling to wake people up and connect them to their true Divine Spirit. There divinely guided people live to help others and work with them to shift to higher emotional states such as love, joy, peace, and compassion while staying away from lower states. Many Empaths identify as being light workers or, indigo's, etc. They achieve their work by spreading their loving energies and dissipating the destructive and negative mass consciousness. This work depends on the light worker learning how to stay centered in love, restraining from Ego and choosing thoughts of love. Using their natural psychic tuning abilities, they can see and feel others' energy centers. They can incorporate psychic healing through this energy work while working with the energy fields of both living and deceased.

Many of the characteristics that are found in Empaths are the same as those used to identify Light Workers. Through an ongoing journey of self-awareness and awakening, you can get in tune with these light-working abilities that you have yet to discover. As they are powerful at manifesting, the main objective should involve self-growth and creating the life you want to live. Their experience is consciously manipulating energy for the purpose of spiritual growth. Not necessarily religious, these types are guided by the spirit realm and are usually considered old souls.

Many Light workers will aim to embrace a global purpose but there is usually a personal agenda that accompanies this. This includes their own conscious expansion through experiences. Like many others in the personal development industry, light workers can recall experiences to help transform and guide others to higher ground.

Dreams

Interpreting dreams to find their relevance in physical life, Empaths often are lucid dreamers. This can be proof of how strong your spiritual side is. This means that there is an ability to shift through dimensions and connect with energies that are beyond the limits of normal understanding.

Free-fall dreams are also common for Empaths. These types of dreams connect with releasing spiritual energies. They also are up to interpretation because many believe that it means strength to stand up for themselves in waking life must be found.

Sequential dreams can be very structured and events in the dreams can be connected. This chronicles events used to bring an understanding of a potential real-life event.

Creative dreams can come across as sources of inspiration. Empaths can get ideas from their dream worlds and bring them into their lives. Having vivid imaginations and lots of experience with multiple forms of energy, Empaths can experience very creative and vivid dream worlds.

Nightmares can be very disturbing and haunting to Empaths. Because they are sensitive beings even the smallest details can settle into a permanent place in their minds until they resolve them. Performing sleep meditations and energy-clearing techniques before resting can help to bring forth positive dreams.

Having the ability to process and deal with the emotional stress that intense dreams can bring forth is important for Empaths. Most of them will be able to define dreams with clarity and understand when their dreams are mirroring their subconscious and spiritual realities.

Before realizing that one is an Empath, it's quite easy for them to go through life as an unsuspecting energy sponge. Those that are unaware of their abilities will take on these emotions and energies everywhere they go without under-standing why. This can lead to suddenly feeling sick or becoming overwhelmed with anxiety or sadness even when there is nothing around to cause this feeling. You must develop specific self-care skills and protection techniques to manage your empathic nature and prevent overload.

Bringing awareness into your body becomes extremely important. Find activities and exercises that bring you back into your body and the present moment. As an Empath, you may experience nervous system overdrive, and it's important that you notice the signs and take the steps to remedy them. Breathing techniques that bring the heart rate down and return to your baseline. Be careful to take stock of how you feel after you spend time with others. It won't take long to learn what people and situations are hazardous to your well-being.

One method of self-care for Living as an Empath is to get in touch with and unblock your chakras. If you are familiar with the 7 Chakras, you understand how you can manage the energy and emotions in your body through them. In just a few minutes a day, you can clear all stored energy and strengthen all these energetic centers. An easy way to do this is to concentrate on a Chakra while meditating and perform breathing exercises, visualizing that you are pulling clear, clean energy into the area and breathing out all negative, and stored energies from the area. There are many stretches that focus on balancing and aligning Chakras, and Yoga can be extremely helpful for Empaths who are feeling overwhelmed. Unblock energies and keep them flowing freely.

Basics of Chakra for Empaths

Root Chakra- (Tailbone Area) The emotional and physical foundations of your life. This is important because the energies of abundance, safety, and stability are held here. The safety and comfort you feel in the world, and the feeling of being taken care of. This includes financial independence, food, and money.

Sacral Chakra- (just above the navel, in the lower abdomen) The creativity, relationships, and passion. Emotional stability, dominant vibrations. This energy center focuses on well-being, sexuality, pleasure, and focus.

Solar Plexus Chakra- (upper abdomen) Governs confidence and empowerment in your life. Helps with acting towards your dreams. This Chakra is possibly the most important for Empaths to focus on. This Chakra governs your guilt/shame dynamic as well as your feeling of worthiness and self-esteem. This is the power center of your body. This chakra helps to direct you to your purpose and path and leads you sources of inspiration.

Heart Chakra- (just above your heart) Energies for joy, love, and inner peace. Connectedness with the world and people, compassion. To practice your ability as an Empath, this Chakra must be well balanced. Your capacity for love, ability to offer empathy, and enjoying inner peace are all connected to this Chakra.

Throat Chakra- (throat) Energies of self-expression, communication, the truth, and feelings. When this Chakra is blocked you may experience an inability to say what you want to say or feel that you are stuck with secrets. For Empaths, emotional honesty is extremely important, and so is taking ownership of your needs in this area.

Brow Chakra- (also known as third-eye chakra located between the eyes) Governs the imagination, the ability to make decisions, wisdom, psychic phenomena and connection to the universe. This Chakra is also important for getting in touch with your intuition.

Crown Chakra- (very top of head) Spirituality and your personal connection to source energy. This includes inner and outer beauty and bliss. It's crucial to creating the life that you love and finding a place of peace. When blocked, the amount of beauty you find in the world, as well as overall feelings of motivation, will decline.

You may encounter people who respond negatively when learning that you're an Empath. Refrain from attempting to convince anyone, it will only cause exhaustion. It's important to note that there are people that have a great aptitude for empathy because they are emotionally intelligent and have a lot of life experience-but they will never identify with any implications of them having abilities that others do not. Find your community, and don't misjudge your own personality. There are just as many people that have vivid extra-sensory experiences of other moods and motivations! Finding your tribe where you belong can help to unload the burdens you'll face. Cultivate those relationships and explore yourself in an understanding and loving environment.

Now that you're beginning to embrace your empathetic side, you need to find the ways that you may have been hiding away from the world because of your sensitivities. You may be skeptical, scared, cautious, and even unconvinced about the need to open to that sensitivity you have. Consciously allow yourself to be vulnerable so that you can begin to reclaim your personal power as an Empath.

Identify Coping Mechanisms

A great way to start training yourself to recognize what your healthy/unhealthy coping mechanisms are is to start a journal. Attempt to identify all of the ways you could be consciously and unconsciously suppressing your empathic abilities. Keep in mind that just because you may have some of the symptoms it doesn't mean that you are repressed, just that you need introspection and examination into why you are experiencing such things. In your journal, start with the following exercise to identify the way you cope with certain people and social situations. To start, make a table with three columns. One each for Physical, Emotional, and Mental. Next, start to list all the forms of suppression you may engage in under each category. Examples of each type are provided.

Physical- Addictions to substances, foods, sex. Isolating yourself. Projecting your energy onto others.

Emotional-Acting one way when you feel differently. Suppressing your feelings or expressing yourself. Exaggerated reactions to loss or trauma. Taking on the role of the martyr.

Mental- Constant criticism or blame. Talking down to yourself of others. Obsessive behaviors. Mental fog, and weariness.

Once you identify the ways that you are currently coping with the energy you meet every day, you can start to work on developing new mechanisms that will help you as you embark on this journey.

Tips for effective living

- Practice allowing yourself to consciously experience your thoughts and emotions, even those that cause discomfort, without any attachments.
- Take time to get to know your thoughts and emotions. You want to get to a point where you can indiscriminately review your thoughts and allow them to pass.
- Identify what you've been telling yourself about the actions of others. Remember that what they do or say reflects their consciousness, not yours.
- Pay attention to your emotions. If you have sudden energy or emotion changes when entering a place or greeting a person, be aware of your part and anyone else's.
- Accept your emotions. Understanding your emotions begins with accepting them. Practice

accepting them as they come and go without stipulation or attachments.

- Identify when the Emotions belong to others. Asses your emotional state before entering a social situation or interaction, and practice disassociating from the emotional state of others.
- Space yourself from the Emotional Energy of others. When you feel physical or emotional changes due to someone else's energy, immediately acknowledge that you don't identify with their emotions.

Once you recognize the situation for what it is, it will be much easier to move away from their state of being. Understanding what tendencies, you may have and working towards healing yourself will aid you in understanding who you really are and how to develop your abilities.

6

Accepting Your Gift

B ecause Empaths are highly sensitive, it's very common
for them to isolate themselves and even unconsciously
hide from their own feelings. The first step in Accepting
your gift of being an Empath is to explore all the ways that
you have both knowingly and unknowingly suppressed your
sensitivities. This is essential in reclaiming your personal
power.

Identify what you are Suppressing

As mentioned in Chapter 4, many Empaths will turn to
various devices of numbing their awareness, and exposure.
How are you numbing yourself? With addictions, depressive
and/or panic disorders, or maybe by completely avoiding
places or people? Eventually, this suppression can take its

toll on your physical, mental, and emotional health. This suppression can manifest itself in many forms.

- **Physical**- excessive sleep /insomnia, shakiness, hypertension, flu-like symptoms, migraines, and chronic fatigue that's unexplained.
- **Emotional**- Anger/Rage Issues, feeling numb, chronic depressive episodes
- **Mental**- Trouble concentrating, negative self-talk, criticizing others

By identifying the ways that you are hiding yourself away and becoming aware of how this is affecting your quality of life, you can begin to release some of the tensions and negative energy that you've been carrying around because of it. Understand and accept that it can be very hard to allow yourself to be vulnerable. It's okay to feel cautious, and skeptical about opening yourself up to those sensitivities. But to avoid living in a state of emptiness, you must consciously allow yourself to be vulnerable.

You have the choice to use your spiritual gift in the service of yourself, others, and humanity in general. Your presence on this planet helps to create some of the highest levels of transformation. The only thing this requires is for you to work on yourself. This should become your major purpose in life- to learn what you need to take care of yourself and nurture your gift. In doing this, you can unlock the ability to not only transform your own life but the lives of others in a profound way. There are even some that believe that Empaths are being incarnated here on earth at this time because it is a time of Transformation!

This can be a big responsibility, and your personal empowerment will help you shoulder it as you move forward. One of the best ways to truly empower yourself is by developing your inherent empathic abilities. A great technique you can use to master your abilities is using the SOAR method. This method is inspired by Zen philosophy and cognitive behavioral therapy related to mindfulness.

- **S- Surrender**

Inhale deeply and relax your body. Allow yourself to feel any tensions or discomforts and take your time to identify what it is you're feeling. Without resistance, consciously surrender them.

- **O-Observe**

Identify and examine the emotions you feel without judging yourself or becoming attached to them. It can be difficult to be an observer of your own feelings but it's necessary to gain control of your thoughts. What attributes can you assign to the feeling? Where does it sit in your body?

- **A-Accept**

Find a place of non-resistance. While processing emotions, it's important to understand that these sensations are temporary. Allow them to come and go.

- **R- Release**

Once you've surrendered yourself to feel the emotions and you've taken the time to observe and examine them as they are passing by, you will notice the feeling associated with the emotions are starting to fade. Release them, even if it requires to go through this process repeatedly.

Develop and Trust Your Intuition

These deep inner feelings that cannot be explained by facts or thoughts are your Intuition. This is not to be confused with Fear. While Intuition is regarded as inner guidance, or internal compass, Fear and negative emotions express themselves through physical responses like racing heartbeat, adrenaline rushes, and aggressiveness. Fear essentially dictates a decision that will make you feel relieved. While a sudden rush of feeling brought on by Intuition can be felt as strongly, it's important to understand the difference. Using your Intuition when you are calm and not in a hurry will allow it to come through. Often, it requires solitude to really slow down and listen to your Intuition.

Be Mindful- The easiest way to practice mindfulness is to focus on the present moment. Develop your own techniques for filtering out all distractions around you and from within. Your Intuition should come through loud and clear.

Notice Patterns- This could be seeing articles about certain subjects repeatedly, or experiencing coincidences concerning an objective you have. It could be having repeated thoughts that seem to come out of nowhere and feeling pulled in certain directions. The last thing you want is to realize your intuition was attempting to speak to you in hindsight.

Go with your Gut-Because your gut is lined with an entire network of neurons, you can experience physical reactions to your emotions and intuition. Our guts are referred to as our "second brain" or the enteric nervous system, having more neurons than our spinal cords and peripheral nervous systems. Have you ever felt physically sick when you've had to make a tough call or realizing you've done the wrong thing? Practice listening to your gut, and interpreting where the feelings are stemming from, and the best way to respond.

Dream it Out- All the information that we experience during the day is processed by our brain in our sleep state. While many dreams are simple scenarios playing out that have no rhyme or reason, dreams can also provide us with information we don't have access to while awake. Meditate on unresolved issues and consider options and emotions before falling asleep. We can pick up on valuable memories, experiences, and learnings by paying attention to where our dreams take us.

Remove yourself from the Situation- Give yourself breathing room. When you find yourself in a tense or uncomfortable situation, creating distance will allow your Intuition to be heard. If something doesn't feel right, it could be time for a change. Get honest with yourself and process your unsettled or unresolved feelings about people or situations. Allow yourself to gain clarity by allowing your mind to rest.

Let Go of Ego- It's also important to distinguish between the times when you are letting your Ego take control. Your Ego can also be known as your rational instinct. It will try to protect you from making mistakes or from failure. While it's useful for helping you survive, you must trust your Intuition to make the right decisions in your life. A good example of this is your instincts telling you to in a job that no longer serves you because it's secure and you feel safe while your intuition may be guiding you towards starting your own business.

Because you're highly sensitive, you can pick up on energies and vibes even when others didn't intentionally share them. Learning to trust your gut feelings and allowing yourself to interpret the messages you receive can help you develop healthy relationships. Learning how to really recognize and listen to your own Intuition will take time. Lead with your heart and trust that you know what choices to make.

You will need to learn ways to avoid taking on other peoples' energy, stress, and symptoms so that you can thrive. The world we live in can sometimes be heartless, insensitive, and coarse. You'll need to work to create a community of support. Remember that Empaths are born, not created. This ability you have allows you to experience depth in life that others do not have access to. This sensitivity permits us to see the beauty in life and allows us to be in service of others.

Once you have done the groundwork for accepting your gift, you've successfully set the stage for now living in your new-found identity. Now it's time to Empower your new life path. What will your purpose of an Empath be? You may feel drawn to help others but fear the emotional exhaustion will affect your ability to function. Rest assured that there are ways to work with people without having to directly deal with the public.

Healing Others

If you are called to healing, you will be sought out by those drawn to the natural Empathic energies that you give off. You can develop your abilities to help heal others' emotional wounds and burdens. You must be prepared to experience the pain of their injuries as psychic pain. Many traditional healers will not have the power to heal emotional traumas, so you may find that you're in high demand.

Though you may deal with painful feelings, it can be

extremely helpful to assist people to simply feel things again. You can use this power to remind others of the good that they've experienced and help them to find ways to be realistic and express gratitude. This allows them to see the silver linings and create a more positive lifestyle.

Understand that you may perform healing energy without being ready, or even wanting to do it. You may experience that you have limited range where you are only effective if you are touching someone.

Empaths are also known as a type of energy - Alchemist. You may be simply talking and resonating with someone and talking with them about the emotions they are experiencing and allowing them to come to their own resolutions. This can be an incredibly healing experience for people. Empaths can transmute and transform the energies they absorb. Take note of the person's demeanor. Body kinetics, facial expressions, and tone of voice all help us to understand others when it comes to their pain and brokenness.

By making it a point to use your ability in the healing of others, you make the decision to live in the open. It's a paranormal ability to apprehend the emotional states of others, and it's okay to let people know about it. This means that you do not have to constantly suppress and shield your sensitivities.

Let go of Insecurities. You will not need to please everyone and it's okay for people to not like you. You don't need to depend on others to have confidence in yourself.

Be Optimistic. If you are experiencing energies while in a state of insecurity, it can drag you down into negativity. You don't need to absorb and hold on to energy, you can simply experience it and understand it before releasing it.

- Let things go. This includes people. It's quite easy to develop "soul ties" as you can experience others pain. This can link souls for longer than you want or expect. You may enjoy the connection at first, but it can turn into unwanted baggage and you must learn to let this go. You must plan an exit strategy so that you do not carry it around with you. Otherwise, your body can turn into a dump for other people.
- Intention and Expectation Setting. Let those you are working with tell you what their expectations are. Ask them their reasons for healing and use that information to set your intentions. When embarking on a new mission of healing, be clear as to *why* you are doing it.
- Establish your Motivation. Why are you drawn to end the suffering of others? Why do you want to aid in their healing? It's not simply because you can do so. You must identify your motivation for each person you meet.
- Invite your Guides. You can ask for the protection

and guidance from guardian angels and spirit guides. You can also invite the person's guide as well - as it will help with directing the healing sessions.

Manifesting

You may be familiar with consciously creating your own reality. There are multiple approaches and theories on the subject, but they all share that our Emotions are a crucial component. Manifesting for Empaths comes with an additional layer of having to sort through which emotions are your and which aren't. Keep in mind that we are *always* manifesting. Because of this, we must be conscious of how and what we are putting out to the universe. Two phrases to guide you on this journey are "know thyself" and "nothing to excess."

For Empaths, knowing yourself will mean that we must be aware of *our* emotional state. Once you've established an emotional baseline you can work on shifting your frequency to more appealing places. If you feel out of alignment with your typical baseline, you now have the desired state to attain.

Focus on what you want, and not what you do not want. Think of things that you wish to attain as if you are already enjoying and experiencing them. Keep in mind the phrase "nothing to excess." Just because a little of something is good doesn't mean that a lot of it will be better.

As Empaths, we tend to swing to extreme sides of every scenario. This includes trying to escape the weight of the world that is on our shoulders. We don't want to feed the mentality of lack, or of not having. This can happen with excessive behaviors. For example, everyone could use more money but is it the money itself or the freedom that money represents that we seek? Putting accurate and realistic attachments to our desires will make manifesting much easier.

By discovering and developing these characteristics, we can use our Empathic abilities to create a better life for ourselves. When we can tune into our own vibrational frequencies, we can easily tune out those that are unwanted or unasked. This can help us from becoming emotionally overwhelmed, overloaded, and exploited. We must fight to maintain a base level of positivity so that our capacity for empathy grows instead of declines.

7

Reaching the Stage of Self-Awareness

Now that you have accepted the gift of being an Empath, it's time to work on becoming self-aware. To understand others, we must understand ourselves. This works in reverse as well. To understand what's going on with the emotions we are picking up from others, we must understand first what emotions are, and where they come from. We also need to learn the distinction between emotions and feelings. Empaths can quickly become emotionally detached, so it's of utmost importance to recognize when this is happening and learn to effectively regulate the emotions we experience.

Emotional Intelligence

Having the mental capacity to precisely perceive, understand, and regulate emotions is critical for empathic skill. This emotional intelligence is a basic understanding that Empaths have meant that emotions aren't simply purely passive behaviors. but ones that can be controlled and managed. That means this reception and transmission of information isn't happening TO us but is something that we are doing ourselves. For an Empath to really understand emotions and simulate another's emotional states they must have a personal interest. The more interest we have, the higher our "action tendency" will be.

Understanding the different types of emotions can help identify why we react the way we do and help us to develop and attune ourselves to them fully. This can be powerful for an Empath who is interested in nurturing their ability and *use* it for the benefit of themselves and others. With Empathic interaction, there are certain techniques we can employ to be intentional. Once practiced, they will seem to run automatically. This intention means that you want to have some level of conscious direction.

The process stages are as follows:

- **Initiation**-This is recognizing the need to impress emotional information both consciously and subconsciously.
- **Selection**-deciding what emotional experience to be impressed and who the subject(s) will be. Getting a basic emotional information impression

- **Induction**-not necessarily hypnotizing someone but rather suggestively impressing upon them emotionally. Focus on reducing discomfort and defining the emotional state of the subject- making that connection.
- **Suggestion-** Compelling the subject to accept the emotional experience. Including direct suggestions or indirect suggestions. This can be done permissively or in an authoritarian manner. Suggesting that emotion be replaced with something positive so that new, positive associations be made the next time they are in the situation.

Emotional Expressions

Knowing the difference between an emotion and a feeling is helpful when identifying and regulating your emotions expressions. A feeling is a required part of an emotion – the component process of emotion. Feeling is just a single component of the emotional experience. In exploring all the types of emotions that we experience from ourselves and others, they can be categorized by a few main types:

- **Utilitarian**-these emotions facilitate our adaptation to events that have consequences regarding our wellbeing and even survival. Many of them being high-intensity crisis reactions.
- **Achievement**- include pride, joy, elation, and satisfaction. For example, Pride in one can trigger

envy or hostility in others. The pride felt collectively can raise a mutually-felt sense of pride, and the enhancement of ego-identity and self-esteem.

- **Approach/Horizon**- relief, hope, surprise, interest. Having the characteristic of positivity and future orientation. Hope plays a vital role in adaptation in pursuing goals. Hope can keep us committed, and motivated and involved. It can also lead to unrealistic or idealistic goals.

- **Resignation**- sadness, fear, shame, and guilt. Characteristically negative and with little control over actions and events They can have positive implications by preventing one from unfavorable risks, they can also result in a decrease in activity and effort.

- **Antagonistic**- envy, disgust, contempt, and anger. Negative, causing enhanced aggressiveness.

- **Aesthetic**-admiration, ecstasy, wonder, harmony

- **Collective/Contagion**-This is the way we compare ourselves to others to assist in determining a label and appropriating emotions. The effect that an Empath has to the bombardment of information is typically based on their level of emotional intelligence and their ability to cope with a situation.

Even more important than understanding and distinguishing between the various types of emotions is our ability to **regulate** them. Regulating emotions is done through various ways including denying, weakening, intensifying, restricting, masking, and/or completely suppressing them. We can modify our emotional reactions and cope with the intensity of a moment and increase our comfort socially. With practice, the most emotionally unregulated Empath can start to develop the bait of regulating emotions effortlessly.

Emotional Regulatory Dysfunctions:

- **Dysregulation-**Emotional evoking events where one can't influence their emotions or adapt them to the social situation. Having poor coping mechanisms such as turning to substance abuse to find relief, can be detrimental to the Empath.
- **Suppression-** concealing or suppressing emotions from others mostly through nonverbal channels. Suppressing an emotion at the moment can be natural, but it must be followed with a somewhat soon reappraisal of those emotions (modifying your view of emotion to lessen its impact)- and processing them. Concealing emotions helps at the moment but can lead to negative effects in the long run.
- **Detachment-** going somewhere else mentally. Making yourself void of emotional response. Not being able to emote freely or practicing this

detachment can lead to emotional disorders related to narcissism. Avoiding certain activities, places, or difficulty loving, bad memory, and paying attention are all effects of this long term.

- **Empathic Fatigue**- Empaths can become increasingly fatigued though empathizing with others-especially those having relationships with dependent people suffering from illness, etc. Those showing the greatest aptitude for empathy typically are prone to this type of fatigue – meaning the larger your capacity for feeling and expressing empathy, the larger the ability for fatigue and stress.

Emotional Regulation Strategies

There are different types of regulation strategies - those occurring before the emotions are encountered, and one after.

- **ANTECEDENT-FOCUSED STRATEGY-** What an Empath does prior to experiencing emotions that can influence their behavior and physiological responses.
- Situation Selection- the first step in this strategy refers to approaching or avoiding certain places, people, things as a means to regulate emotions. If you know or speculate that emotions will be

triggered in a certain situation, you have the option to avoid it altogether or approach it in a way that will allow you to regulate the influx of feelings and emotions it will bring forth.

- Situation Modification- Changing a situation to soften its emotional impact-also known as primary control or problem focusing on coping. Choosing how an interaction will take place for the benefit of both parties. If someone asks you to talk with them about a delicate situation but you are suffering from burnout or overstimulation-you would want to arrange a time to discuss the situation with them when you have the mental capacity to create positive outcomes.

- Attention Deployment- Focusing on certain aspects of a situation. Could be the big picture, or the positive aspects of a distressing situation, or distracting themselves from a conversation they find stressful and thinking about something else. Either something that exists in the situation or something as simple as counting numbers or thinking of pleasant memories. "going to your happy place"

- Cognitive Change- used to decrease emotional response. Telling yourself "it's only their opinion, and "that's not necessarily true" This is reflected in changing emotions such as anger towards a criminal to pity.

- **RESPONSE-FOCUSED STRATEGY - The** steps an Empath can take once an emotion is being experienced. This includes remaining impartial to an emotion or thoughts and feelings associated with it. It also includes actively allowing yourself to feel those associations to fully release them once experienced.

- **RESPONSE MODIFICATION - Influencing** emotional response -typically by suppressing emotions through reappraisal. Looking at emotion in a non-emotional way. This can lead to deception and takes a large amount of both psychological and physiological energy to sustain. You're basically nipping emotion in the bud.

- **ENERGETIC-REGULATION STRATEGY -** using physical exercise to regulate emotion. This strategy shows that Empaths that remain physically active will have an easier time regulating emotions due to the automatic neurochemical alterations that happen because of that regular exercise.

Processing Emotions

There are three main stages of emotional processing. When you are being mindful, and intentionally identifying and processing your emotions it can help to have a process in place so that you don't get lost and spend too much time dwelling on something that can be revisited later.

• Initiation

Recognizing the need for sharing an emotional experience both consciously and subconsciously. Focusing on the need or stating the need. Empaths can be filled with apprehension and uncertainty and will need to dismiss those feelings to initiate the empathic processes.

• Physical Interaction

Physically interacting with a subject or group. Required for tele-empathy. This takes the empaths simulation above and beyond what can be done through a quantum state. This can be talking, being in one's physical presence or physically touching them. This interaction causes a type of entanglement to better share the emotional information.

• Psychophysical Interaction

This refers to how the shared emotional information is measured. This is basically taking all the information you are being given and creating one definite classical emotional state from that information. This can take a while especially if the emotional states of the subject are continuous. Once you achieve this stage you simultaneously simulate each other's emotions. This can lead to similar behaviors.

When you can identify the emotions and energies that you are receiving, you will better understand how to respond to them and process them. This is beneficial not only for your well-being but in the healing assistance of others. Untrained Empaths can commonly be received as cold and distant because they tend to shut out all input. This can make you see as if you care less about the problems being presented to you. Even coming from this defensive state, we can learn to overcome by accepting the gifts we are given and attuning ourselves. Once you are better able to control the energies, keep in mind that you can still come across as unfeeling and suppressive. Empaths must take care of their passions as they can become overwhelming. We can develop a logical manner of looking at life to handle the onslaught of emotion. This will require a serious discipline of the mind as there is a fine line between emotional isolationism and self-discipline.

. . .

Living from the Heart

Now that you are familiar with your Heart Chakra, and how to clear any energies stored there you can invite energy of protection and healing in. Maintaining an open heart is a physical process that you must work on. This means that even when faced with adversity, or someone else's low vibes, you don't close off your heart you open it further.

When we are living from our Hearts it means that we stop allowing our mind to dominate our lives. This means that we stop compartmentalizing everything we meet in our environments into neatly labeled concepts. We can work on adding to this all or nothing attitude and rigid thinking. Through a mind-dominated life, we stop seeing others as expressions of divine energy. We lose our courage to be vulnerable and we wear masks that can suffocate. Commit to living with your heart open so that you can truly start your journey of self-awareness and spiritual practice.

Imagine the heart as a doorway to the Soul. Love itself is the reward we receive for opening our Hearts and accessing our strongest forces. This also allows for healing to take place. Healing of all that you've experienced and suffered as well as everything yet to come. When you open your heart, you have access to the eternal, and the present moment.

- **Silence**- Disconnect yourself from all sources of

stimulation so that you have no distractions. This solitude can open the space you need to listen to your true self. In doing this you are setting the stage and environment to explore your heart.

- **Comfort**- Find a mantra or affirmation that brings you peace and comfort. Your inner child resides in your Heart and opening it up you may find that you feel like a scared child. Encourage yourself and your heart to open more deeply by providing yourself with things that bring you comfort.

- **Feel**- With permission to feel you receive permission to grow. When our hearts are closed it is usually because we deny and suppress certain emotions and feelings. Allow yourself to investigate what you've put away and give yourself permission to access and process these feelings.

- **Connect**- When opening your heart with the intention of living from it you have access to true unconditional love. This is the presence that is watching over that inner child there. This force is supportive and maintains its presence even in front of all our pain. We must allow this parental force to emerge from our hearts and fill us with the knowledge that nothing we have ever done or could do will influence this unconditional love.

- **Breathe**- It can be overwhelming when you are accessing intense feelings and suppressed emotions. Practice deep breathing techniques to connect you to your body. You should feel this sort of congested energy start to leave your body as you align your energy. As you process and release these emotions and feelings you should start to feel a new space in yourself. Breathe positive energy into this space and honor the emotions that have just been released.

- **Pray**- This includes stating your intentions to attract guidance and support. This isn't necessarily a religious act- as you can pray to whom or whatever you resonate with, even life itself. This practice can open your heart because when we are sincere and humble, we can more readily receive guidance. Identify and release any prejudices you may have towards praying. You open yourself up to immense growth when you communicate with a universe that is always listening.

- **Put in the Work**- This means that we may experience feeling uncomfortable. Our aversion to discomfort leads to a closing of our hearts but we must realize it can be extremely valuable. Take note of what we are reacting to, even negatively. There is much to learn from the things we run away from. Embrace the feeling and be receptive so that you can process and release these emotions. You're working on adopting a new mindset that means being receptive, not reactive.

- **Allow yourself to Cry**- Allowing ourselves to be overcome with emotion is difficult for almost everyone. Empaths can be so emotionally congested that even simply crying at all can be difficult. Give yourself privacy, and experience things that make your heart stir. Fight the emotional stiffness you may feel and remember that expressing emotion in this way is normal and it's something that we need to honor.

- **Ask your Heart**- Learn to engage with your heart and what it needs. This is best done in silent stillness. It's easy for our hearts to be drowned out by day to day life so take the time to ask what you need. Ask your heart how you can feel better. Ask whatever questions may come naturally. Answers may come through physical sensations or visualizing words. Being receptive takes practice but can provide a great amount of guidance.

- **Be Vulnerable**- When we open ourselves we acknowledge that we are exposing ourselves. This fear of vulnerability kicks in our instincts to do whatever we can to defend ourselves against attack. While we can't force ourselves to be vulnerable, we can sort of coax ourselves into more and more vulnerable states. Find a sense of security within yourself that you can take the needed risks when opening your heart.

- **Shut down the Critic**- Disregard the inner critic that can convince you that you're doing something stupid or even wrong. That critic wants us to believe that we are making a fool of ourselves. Recognize when this critic is speaking to you and treat it with love. Once you can see it for what it is we recognize it's usually a lonely voice crying out for love and attention.

Opening your heart means that you are going to be processing your innermost private thoughts and feelings. Practice opening your heart to people in your life. Try opening it to new situations, or spaces where you have closed yourself off.

Cultivating Peace

As Empaths we have a responsibility to ourselves and others to find the tools we need, create the space we will flourish in, and find a community that we can lean into. By practicing peace, we can ground ourselves from moment to moment. This will allow you to be in alignment with what peace is for you. There are easy ways to cultivate more peace in our lives such as finding ways to laugh, listening to music, donating your time and/or money, staying in contact with people, limiting negative self-talk, and setting and respecting your boundaries. There are common ways to practice cultivating peace:

- Release- Learn to release attachment to everything. This includes your own comfort and situations. Some things will be difficult to release but you must question old ways of being to see if they are currently serving you. You cannot live abundantly without letting go of the grasp you maintain and the control you have over certain parts of your life.

- Fear- Learn to face your fears. Open yourself up to self-discovery and investigate where you might be avoiding or ignoring your own fears. Once you identify them, work on tearing them apart piece by piece. Then work on releasing them and changing your patterns so that you can cultivate a life that is in alignment with your needs and desires. You can claim your power and dictate how you move around, and through your fears. Just this practice alone will bring forth a great sense of peace.

- Trust- Learn to trust your own heart. When we are disconnected from our true selves we become cut off from what our hearts are telling us. Remember that your peace is your top priority so learn to listen to your inner voice. This can be hard for us when that voice doesn't match up with the expectations you have for yourself, or it's different from what others may think of you. You intuitively know what deserves your energy and what does not, listen to your heart.

- Forgive- Learn to forgive yourself and others. This means being accountable for yourself and holding others accountable. Forgiving them simply means that you no longer allow your, or others, pain to take up space in your life. The peace that brings will help you realize that your own actions are no longer being led by the feelings associated with not forgiving someone. This opens space for more good in your life.

- Remember- Learn to remember your true essence. This doesn't mean what you are doing and who you are doing it with. This is a remembering of the fact that you are filled with peace, that you are powerful, and that you are a manifestation of divine energy. When you find yourself questioning yourself and your direction, take the time to reconnect to your truth. Cultivate peace by projecting that image of yourself.

Cultivating peace is a practice. It's a decision that we make every day, from moment to moment. It will look differently everyday but if you remain committed to it you will create more space in your life for joy, love, and peace.

8

Grounding Techniques to Help You Center Yourself

When we are ungrounded, uncentered, and disconnected from the Earth we can be distracted easily. We also tend to space out, over-think things, engage in drama, and experience anxiety. Being obsessed with your personal image, being easily deceived, and possessing a desire for material things are signs of being off center and out of alignment. This can manifest physically with inflammation, fatigue, chronic pain, poor sleep, and poor circulation.

When you are centering or grounding yourself, remember there is no right or wrong way of doing things. You simply need to find ways that are effective for you to get in touch with the earth and your surroundings, as well as with your-self. Using meditative visualizations are a great way to powerfully reinforce your connections. When you choose to use grounding is up to you. Whether it's in preparing for events ahead of time or to unwind after experiences. You can even find these beneficial if you're simply feeling ill, have experienced trauma, or just want to feel more centered.

When we are grounded we are fully present in our bodies and/or feeling connected to the earth.

Grounding

Grounding can help to clear your mind, recharge your ener-gies, strengthen your intuition and instincts, and calm your emotions. These techniques are designed to help redistribute the energy from your head into your body and can have an almost instant calming effect. The more rooted we are in our bodies, the less stress and anxiety we will experience. Being fully present in our bodies and feeling connected to the earth will allow us to focus on our empathic abilities and be in the service of others.

There are basic steps you can take to ground yourself. Connecting to your natural environment, finding ways to recharge your batteries, and practicing being mindful are great places to start. Follow the steps below to ground yourself:

- **Cover your Crown**- Place one hand over the crown of your head and simply hold it there for a minute. This brings an awareness of your physical and spiritual bodies that you are held here.

- **Feel your Feet**- Bring all your awareness to the bottom of your feet. Pay attention to any sensations you come across there. Visualize your awareness moving across your foot up through your ankle, and feel how they connect you to the physical Earth.

- **Follow your Breath**- Trace the air as you breathe in and out. Follow the air as it enters your body, taking a moment to notice the feeling on your nose and mouth, down your throat and into your lungs. Practice this technique and observe your breathing. Let your body lead the way and allow your mind to simply observe.

- **Be A Tree-** Stand like a tree by placing your feet shoulder width apart. Tuck your chin into your chest and sink all your weight to your feet. Visualize all your weight being absorbed into the ground. This can be a powerful visualization for grounding.

- **Cold Showers-** Being able to take a cold shower is an invigorating experience. Start by turning the water slightly cooler towards the end of your shower for progressively longer periods of time with colder water. This can bring your awareness into your physical body and increase your feeling of being connected to this Earth.

- **Visualize Heat-** A simple visualization for this would be to visualize a volcano. Focus on the Orange and Red spectrum of color. Visualize the molten lava that's deep within the earth, always in motion. Picture it is moving upwards towards you, erupting like a volcano into your body. Envision that you are absorbing the energy in the lava as it invigorates and strengthens you. Hold this power and understand that it's accessible to you whenever you may need it.

- **Check your Posture**- Recognize your bodily mannerisms. Locate sources of tension and stress in your body. Create an exercise of awareness starting with your feet and work your way up through the top of your head, releasing any of the tension you come across.

- **Eat Well**- Adapt to a diet that includes roots, herbs, and minerals. Adopt the properties of the foods you ingest. This means staying away from processed foods and potentially refraining from any food that was created in a non-consensual manner.

Earthing

In theory, Earthing allows a transfer of negatively charged electrons from the Earth's surface into the body, therefore, neutralizing positively charged free radicals that can cause chronic inflammation. Think about how the tires on your car can prevent lightning in a storm. Now imagine how the rubber soles on your shoes are affecting your body's electro-magnetism. Earthing can be simple to do. Any earth, grass, stone, or sand can provide the natural environment you need to Earthing. Standing, walking or lying down on these surfaces will increase the awareness of the Earth beneath us. Researchers in the Earthing movement suggest staying bare-foot for at least 20 minutes twice a day but we should do this as much as we can every day.

Methods for Earthing:

- **Mindful Walking -**This refers to walking while staying present with your natural environment. Within minutes you should feel more mentally calm and centered. Go barefoot if you can as this can massage acupuncture points in your feet as you would find in reflexology. Bring awareness to the steps you take, and the weight in them.

- **Roll like a Cat**- Imagine that you are discharging negative energy (because you literally are!) and roll around as a cat or dog would. Maybe as a child, you rolled down a big hill at the park- see if you can create space for yourself to do this. Being playful in nature is key to Earthing and connecting.

- **Stand like a Tree**- Just as in grounding, do this barefoot and out in the open air. Bring awareness to how you are rooted to the earth but notice that you have free will regarding where you remain.

- **Visualize**- Center yourself and focus on your heart. Be present with the energy of life that's emanating from it. Imagine the center of the earth is a circle of light or core of magma. Visualize a beam of light or energy going form your heart all the way down to the earth's core. Visualize another beam coming from the core of the earth directly to your heart- feel the connection between your heart and the earth's core for a few minutes.

The methods will increase your awareness of your body. There is a wide range of positive health benefits achieved by performing these techniques. Reforming your connection to the earth will help to quiet and clear your mind, recharge your energy and calm your emotions. This will increase your overall physical and mental performance which is essential for any Empath that is attuning to others. Use these grounding techniques to help awaken your instincts and bring you even closer to yourself.

. . .

Centering

Feeling off center is very similar to feeling ungrounded or disconnected. When you are in the Center of your awareness and energy, you will feel no resistance. You allow yourself to be active, alert, and alive. When you are centered, your inner calm takes over and allows you to act spontaneously. Keep in mind that in the Center, you are neutral.

Signs that you are off center will include not knowing the difference between what's important and what's urgent. Constantly checking your watch, or email and phone throughout the day. Being consumed with negative self-talk, and having a hard time focusing on the task at hand. If you're feeling stuck or overwhelmed it may be that you are off center.

Keeping yourself centered also means letting go of your Ego. Balancing your Ego and your Spiritual side should be something you work on every day. Put yourself around people that compliment your own energy. Work to create an inner harmony that cannot be influenced by the energies of those around you. Consider your workspace. Is it making you happy? Is it serving you? If not, you should make the necessary changes to remove this toxicity from your life.

The connection you maintain is your responsibility. When we are center, we connect with our instincts and true feelings. In addition to the steps outlined for Grounding and Earthing, you should add the following:

- **Establish Levels-** The plumb line in our bodies is completely straight and vertical. Find your plumb line by letting your eyes fall to the tip of your nose. Then direct your awareness towards your third eye region, the center of your forehead just an inch or so above your eyebrow line. This can take practice, but you will feel once you've established this plumb line. Realize that you can access it whenever you need to center yourself quickly.

- **Become an Observer-** Seek higher ground by placing your awareness a few inches above the crown on your head. Be a casual observer of any feelings, thoughts, and sensations from this vantage point. This can provide space between you and any drama that your Ego is bringing forth. Maintain this perspective for as long as you are comfortable.

To maintain being centered, try lots of different ways of feeling connected and reconnecting yourself. Keep yourself curious and practice while maintaining innocence. Our center holds a powerful point of equilibrium that we can access to bring us into the present moment. Once you've mastered centering yourself, you will be able to do so with just a few breaths.

Emotional Calibration

When we calibrate our emotions, it allows us to make better choices of ourselves and allows us to become more effective communicators. As Empaths, it allows us to be even clearer about what we are feeling for ourselves, and what is coming from the environment around us.

Just as it is with clinicians and health professionals, we can use this emotional calibration to make our intentions and intuitions explicit. This self-control over our emotions will have influence over our decision making and our feelings of indulgence and restraint.

One of the best ways to re-calibrate your emotions is by simply taking a break and doing something that brings you joy. This means making a commitment to joyful living and making yourself take the time to do the things that you find enjoyable. We must be intentional with our time. This doesn't have to mean directly work and play. It comes down to what is giving you life and what is draining your life. Make room for the things that fulfill you.

Find ways that you can develop yourself through new interests. Integrate the emotions you feel with reason. This can help your emotions from running all over the place unchecked. This can help guide you when making important decisions.

Decompress

End with Wine- After a workday it can be beneficial to consume a glass of red wine. There have been many studies recently into the antioxidants and overall benefit of one glass of wine a day. Remember to drink water before and after, and to not drink to excess.

Vision Board/Dream Book- Take time to focus on your future. If you're not familiar with creating a vision board, simply cut out images and words that are aligned with what you desire for your future self. This could be material things such as cars, and a new home but also images and words that evoke feelings within you that you want to manifest. Dream Books are essentially the same as vision boards, but they are meant to be updated and kept as a journal. Make daily updates to stay in alignment.

High Impact Exercise- Investigate taking a boxing class, or a spinning class if you are able. Whatever will be high impact for you, swimming laps as fast as you can or some sort of exercise that allows you to work through any aggression you may be holding onto. You'll find that it's much easier to decompress from your day if you leave things behind at a workout session.

In addition to these simple everyday tasks, there are different types of therapies that can be extremely beneficial for Empaths that need to Decompress from their daily life.

Candle Therapy

This naturopathic practice is gaining popularity as of late. Sensory candle therapy is referring to different colors and fragrances of candles that you burn and meditate on to bring forth the magical powers in your life. Many spirit workers use many different colors for different types of fertility, divination, and prosperity. Separate from the colors of the Chakras, the metaphysical properties affected use a much broader range of color.

Traditionally used to unite the powers of spirit, body, and mind, candle therapy is a great practice to start during your transition as an Empath. Closely aligned with energy work, it uses the mind as a powerful tool in creating bridges between what we desire and ourselves. In relation to vibrational energy, the color chosen will have a resonating value that you should want to work with. This makes for a potent catalyst for manifesting things in your life.

There are many configurations for candles that will have certain effects. Balancing, connecting, mediumship, etc., are directly related to the layout of candles. Learn about creating a higher vibrational spiritual field for yourself.

. . .

Aromatherapy

Aromatics have been in used since ancient times across the globe. This includes burning resins, plant roots, and barks. In modern time we learned to distill the plant matter into essential oils. These oils contain the therapeutic properties of the plant and can aid you on your spiritual journey as well as help you to stay in alignment with divine energy. These oils, when inhaled, can disinfect our raspatory systems, act as decongestants and provide mental health benefits. The molecules that enter into our olfactory system and in turn, our limbic system have an effect on our emotions, stress levels, and general well-being.

You may be drawn to certain scents or blends. Certain scents will have different effects on you physically and mentally. You'll want to experiment with things until you identify what works best for you. If you want to increase your contentment, try lavender and/or rosemary. If you're more interested in staying alert reach for peppermint. Lemon and other citrus oils are great for stress relief and focus.

Water Therapy

This includes simply Getting in the water! Washing your hands with natural soaps or taking a long bath or hot shower to get some of the daily energy off you can be a great way to decompress. Put your well-being first by making time for yourself to enjoy the water. For Empaths, spending time in and around water can be calming and rejuvenating. Go to the beach, take a hike next to a lake, play in the rain, go for a swim, and find ways to immerse yourself in water. Enjoy the buoyancy of water and the freedom from gravity's effects on our bodies.

Stay hydrated! We are made of water and water passes through us, cleaning out toxins as it travels. Add citrus to provide antioxidants and flavor. Respect your body and give it what it needs to function at maximum capacity.

Now that you have exercises and a basic understanding of how to ground yourself and keep you at your center, you'll want to practice maintaining this state. Start by owning the moment you are in. This moment you are in right now is the most important moment and nothing outside of it should have any influence. Remember to take control of your emotions. You're responsible for the way you respond to situations so remember that you are always in charge of them. Keep in mind that it's important to make time for others. Step outside of your own perspective and struggles and use your empathic abilities to reach out to those around you.

Create a routine for yourself. It's easy to become ungrounded when we are multitasking and being pulled in multiple directions at once. Create a routine for certain parts of your day and stick to it. This could be as simple as starting every day with making your bed. No matter what happens during your day after that, you know that you will return home to a made bed. Knowing that you accomplished that easily and basically effortlessly will encourage that behavior for the rest of your day.

9

Blocking Out the Unwanted
Emotions of Others

How can Empaths enjoy normal activities and lead fulfilling lives if they are always battling the constant over-stimulation? By trusting their instincts, setting boundaries for themselves and others, and practicing ways to block out the incoming information until they can be receptive to it.

Use the methods found in Chapter 6 for developing your Intuition. Use it in the way you filter the world around you, and how you relate to it. Pay attention to social cues and the emotions of those around you and practice saying to yourself "This energy and emotion is not mine. I ask it to be released from me immediately." When you give yourself this power to dismiss the unwanted or unsolicited emotion, you can more easily interact with things without attachment.

Even television programs, movies, news broadcasts, and social media updates can bring an Empath to experience traumatic emotional discomfort levels. Many Empaths will have a hard time comprehending cruelty and needless suffering. We can always find ways to deal with and work on overcoming depression, anxiety, and being too sensitive to other's emotions. During this type of spiritual awakening, there can be waves of emotions that are new and it can be hard to communicate and stay in control. Disorienting and feeling like you have just stepped out of a cave, this awakening can be overwhelming.

There are steps you can take to create the balance you will need. Start with honoring where you are in this moment, and then set energetic boundaries for yourself and others. Learn to recognize when you're overstimulated, practice calming your nervous system, and finally practice using visualization techniques to really block out those unwanted and intrusive energies.

Honor Where You Are Now

Accept that you're feeling so sensitive because of the path you are on. Give yourself the time and space for self-care. It's easy to live in denial, but with self-love and nurturing for yourself and this path you are on, you can empower yourself to use your abilities. Do this for yourself. Accept that you may not be feeling ideal and that you have some things to work on. By honoring who and where you are now you can develop powerful techniques that help keep you centered.

- **Create Space**- Have a place that you can retreat to. Create an ideal circumstance for yourself. Recuperate. Set your boundaries. Quietness and low stimulation are ideal. Let your energy and senses spread out without intrusion. Do this as often as possible so that you can feel better. Make the choice to fit this into your life.

- **Reach out for Support**- Knowing that you are not alone is extremely comforting. Even just one person that you can engage with can make huge improvements in feeling alone. What you're going through is real and it can be difficult. You are not alone. There are forums, and resources online so that you can connect digitally to other Empaths that are on the same journey.

- **Go with the Flow**- Don't expect an easy ride. There is a natural progression to your journey, though it may hardly seem like it. Act on your intuition to make fast progress. You will be able to find joy, and passion and excitement and adventurous life. You must create your own path and take the steps that present themselves to you as you go. Justify acting on situations based on your intuition

- **Shadow Work**- The way you feel are clues to resolving your issues and grow. Depression, anxiety, and other issues can correlate to your inner issues and can be a mirror for you to examine where you need to focus your attention. You can dramatically improve your life and feel renewed when you find ways of healing yourself. This could be grounding exercises such as yoga or meditation, or spiritual retreats. Bring awareness to these pockets of energy in your body and life. Find what you are naturally attracted to. Solutions will find you, but you must be able to accept them. Take the time to do the inner work and find out where these issues are stemming from. Your inner being will guide you into healing.

Accepting and owning that being an Empath is a part of

your life can bring significant positive changes. It may mean potentially humbling yourself but know and honor that you will need to make time for yourself, have safe spaces, take frequent breaks, and that sometimes you will just have to say no.

Set Energetic Boundaries

Don't be afraid to say no. Doing so is not necessarily negative, it's assertive. By knowing what you want and taking a moment to look within we can identify why we are feeling certain ways and find any unresolved issues within ourselves. Everyone we deal with is a mirror of what we need to work on in ourselves. Take the actions to protect and heal yourself. After all, *you* are the one putting yourself out there.

- **Connect**- Connect with those who remind you of who you are. Make time to connect and harmonize with nature. Remind yourself that every one that is coming into your life is doing so to teach you more about yourself. No one can permeate your awareness without your invitation because you hold the power to accept. You must take responsibility for your internal connection and liberate yourself. Take the time to create the boundaries you will use when connecting to yourself. Express and employ these boundaries while purposefully seeking out connections with others.

- **Self-Focus**- There is no need for you to experience feelings that don't belong to you unless you want to. By directing your focus inward and becoming aware of how you feel in certain situations, you can begin to determine where your feelings end, and another begins. Create mental boundaries so that you can block out incoming messages.

- **Shielding**- Come up with an energy ritual for yourself. This could be a visualization technique you use to protect your energy. Imagine that by just having a thought you can activate an energetic shield that protects your energy on the inside and keeps all other energies out. This is quick and simple to perform daily, or prior to entering a social situation. Another visualization trick that many Empaths employ is to create a cord that connects them to the core of the earth, grounding you there so that you are connected even when you are not allowing incoming energies.

- **Express your Needs**- This is especially true for asserting your needs in relationships. You must be comfortable enough to raise issues with someone if you feel that something isn't right. You can start by asking yourself what you need in a relationship to feel protected. This is also true in workspaces, or other social situations where you can receive accommodations. No one will know what you need until you tell them. Set your energetic boundaries at home and at work. Surround yourself with objects that bring you calm, use noise-canceling headphones, and whatever you need to protect your energy levels.

Recognize Overstimulation/Calming your Nervous System

There are common signs and symptoms of overstimulation. Physically, you may experience lightheadedness, chronic headaches, racing thoughts, lost interest in things you typically enjoy, avoiding being touched, insomnia, agitation, and many others. Understand that you're not alone in dealing with sensory overload. Refrain from comparing yourself to those that are not highly sensitive since we have established that our brains and systems work differently.

Start to take notice of areas that are highly stimulating for you- the mall, birthday parties, amusement parks, traffic jams, etc. Plan your day or week with these spaces in mind. If you must participate in these types of activities, be sure that you're not doing so back-to-back. Decide what is worth it to you regarding putting yourself out there.

Be mindful of how much time you spend in front of a screen. Any digital screen will tax your senses and over time, lead to overstimulation. Small changes can help you battle overstimulation. It could be that you always wear sunglasses outside, that your wardrobe for work consists of natural, breathable clothing. Check the dim settings on your home-land, work lighting if you can. Wear headphones when in public, or at work if you can.

Calming Your Nervous System

Because you are fundamentally highly-attuned to the energies around you, it's easy to be depleted. When you add in predatory energies to the equation, it can often be debilitating. This would include habitual complainers, emotional vampires, narcissists, etc. You must regulate your nervous system so that any issues you experience on a physiological and spiritual level will not manifest negatively in your life. Chronic fatigue, unexplained aches and pains, and environmental sensitivities have all be contributed to outside influences.

Mitigate the impact of these types of energies by becoming aware of and working to balance your nervous system.

- **Track your Stress Responses**

Alarm Stage/Phase-This is when your nervous system goes into "fight or flight" mode. This is the opposite of our natural state known as "rest and digest." This can be brought on by physical or emotional pain, or with the learning new information suddenly. In this phase, you produce massive amounts of adrenaline to deal with the perceived threat or issue. When the trigger is ongoing such as being in an abusive relationship, mismanagement of finances, etc., it can instantly progress into the second stage.

Resistance Stage/Phase- Getting locked into a negative cycle of dealing with stress causes your body to produce high levels of Cortisone. This can have various negative effects on your quality of life and health when it's a chronic experience. Physically you may experience muscle loss, producing fewer neurotransmitters like serotonin, and various digestive problems.

Exhaustion/Burnout Stage/Phase-When dealing with the increased adrenaline and internal stimulation that comes with traditional stress responses over a long period of time, you will most certainly experience adrenal, mental, emotional, and physical fatigue. In addition to the physical symptoms mentioned in stage 2, this exhaustion stage can make you listless, and cause you to develop apathetic and cynical outlooks. It can cause disruptive sleep patterns and an irregular state of functioning.

Seek calming, sedative support. Locate minerals and herbs that promote balance and calm. Locate a therapist so that you can talk things out. Begin to bring yourself back into a regulated state. Surround yourself with people that love you and emit the same frequency or higher energy than ourselves. Start to determine how the energy of other people and situations is serving you. Remember, it's okay to only feel the energies, you don't have to *become* them.

• **Relax the Nervous System Naturally**

Get Active- Be active. The more you move into your body the more you're free yourself. You are giving energy and creating it rather than sucking it up like a sponge.

Laugh- You may have heard that laughter is the best medicine, and that's because it gets us out of our stressed states and helps us release some of the tension and even physical pain that we carry.

Eat Well- When we give our bodies what they need to function at an optimal level, we allow our nervous system to perform its job from a state of rest. Be sure to nourish your body properly. Pay attention to the amount of magnesium and be mindful of how much protein you take in. Make a point of hydrating daily with pure water.

Focus on your Breath- Breathe with your gut. Fill your lungs completely and hold the air with your belly. Push all the air out fully before taking another inhalation. Do this for a minute or so to get instant relief from nervous states. Focus on an affirmation or mantra while practicing.

Meditate- Mindfulness meditations with calming visualizations can keep your nervous system calm. Practice deep breathing and look for ways to relax. Remember that whatever we focus on grows so be mindful of where you are placing your attention. Do not give your attention to things that are not serving you, but rather the things that you love.

Visualization Techniques for Blocking

As mentioned in the Shielding technique, visualization is a quick and efficient way to mentally protect yourself. In addition to the ways we can create a shield for ourselves to block out unwanted energies and emotions, we can practice visualization when we want to connect, block out, or disconnect from them as well. Below are a few types of visualizations that can help with blocking:

Insulation- In this type of visualization, you'll want to picture your energetic connections as hollow tubes, or small straws, poking out of your skin. Imagine pulling these tubes back inside, closing them off. This could also be imagined as being inside of a geodesic dome that has windows open. Simply visualize that you are closing those windows and in turn, blocking out any energy from getting inside.

Heating with Light- Visualize that there is a light inside of you just strong enough to make you faintly glow. When you feel unwanted energies, imagine them as being a different color of light. Focus on your energy, your light, pushing the others away or dissolving them. Use the heat from your light to vaporize the incoming energies.

Spirit Animal- This can work for you if you envision an animal that you can call forth the spirit to protect you. Visualize the animal, typically a wolf, jaguar, or another animal that you may have a spiritual connection to. In your mind's eye, see how the animal patrols your energy field and protects it. Give thanks to the animal and know that you can call on it whenever you need.

You will want to sometimes purposefully connect with energies for co-creating or healing. You want to be mindful of withdrawing your connection every time you are done. You don't want to leave gaps in your shielding and blocking. To do this, you can simply reverse a visualization you used to connect to the energy.

Understand that you will need to find ways healthy ways to cope with everyday life. Blocking out the feelings and emotions of others can make Empaths appear reclusive and sometimes unresponsive. Sometimes they can even appear ignorant as they can shut down as a defense mechanism.

You may notice that you tend to project the feelings you pick up from others back onto them without even realizing it. Maybe you bottle up all the motions and that leads to crippling or explosive outbursts. Empaths are prone to ignoring their own needs while focusing on others.

Follow these steps and techniques to prevent yourself from burning out and suffering from complete mental exhaustion. If you are mindful of your baseline emotions, it will help you to recognize when there are other energies coming into your focus. Maintaining that energetic boundary around yourself will help you deflect anything you are not ready to experience and process. Remember to focus your awareness where you want your energy to flow! This is one of the most important considerations for Empaths.

10

Overcoming Your Fears,
Grasping Your Power, and
Nurturing Your Empathic
Abilities

E mbrace the Paradigm Shift

On your journey as an Empath, you will realize that a positive, and optimistic paradigm shift is happening in your existence. Act to embrace this new learning. We can lose ground by waiting until the time is right, or when certain aspects of our lives are where we want them to be. You must decide to shape your future now. This can be challenging but can have huge rewards and opportunities in this redesigning and alignment of your life.

Work to align your emotional awareness and your physical body. This can take the form of small, everyday improvements such as extending your awareness to other and working on processing any suppressed emotions. Many of the experiences you will go through aren't easily explained with the language we have now. Embracing the unknown and the shift on traditional paradigms will help you be successful.

Keep in mind that paradigm shifts apply to everything in our lives. The shift is constant and much of it will go on unrecognized and even internalized. It can depend on how receptive you are to change. Keep an open mind for "a-ha" moments. Even just reading this book could be one of the first "a-ha" moments you experience in a long line of them in your self-journey.

Note all the ways you bring suffering to yourself. At what points of your day is negative self-talk more likely? Do you let it run rampant when you're doing the dishes? Once you realize the first negative thing you say to yourself in the day-stop it in its tracks. The next day, it should be easier to correct yourself into positive thinking patterns. Practice this every day, and every time you notice automatic negative thoughts.

Recognize that by bringing awareness to your life experience you open it up to the possibility of change. Identify patterns that we do not wish to perpetuate. Respond to these in life-affirming ways. Refuse to live a life ruled by unconscious motives and habits. They are in our control, we just need to take the time to surface them and identify them.

Examine your reactions and look inward. We cannot control how others act so we must relinquish the thought of having control over them. Investigate why you need to control how they react and do it with compassion for yourself. Understand yourself and empower your freedom. Examine your thoughts about the past, and your future. You may notice that many of them are based on fear or the lack of things you want and need. Be in the present moment and refrain from feeding anything outside of this moment our attention.

The shift from Judgement and Criticism to a place of Appreciation and Gratitude. It can take a long time to keep critical thoughts under control. With this practice, you will become more open and available naturally. Practice by verbalizing your appreciation and love for your friends and family, and even to strangers.

Becoming a Skilled Empath

Be Conscious

This means being deliberate in how you react to situations, how people make you feel, and how you interact with the world at large. Be Conscious of your energies so that you can heal anything that's accumulated. Deliberately develop your skills so that they will be of service to you. Take responsibility for your own influence. How you are impacting others is just as important as how they affect you.

Be Present

That means being present, and at the moment when

working with your own energies and with others. It is easy to be misunderstood and assume that others disapprove of us. Understand that being an Empath is a normal human trait, a gift that you have been given. Do not allow your attention to be drawn away or impeded when you are focusing on your own or others energy work.

Do not Assume

We can make mistakes by making assumptions on our observations. As an Empath, you know that feeling something physically and feeling something mentally are completely different aspects that come with their own sets of complications. Focus your attention on what feelings may be trying to reveal to us. If you know something, or that something is about you can be detrimental to your growth.

Sculpt your Emotional Landscape

Nurture the emotions and states of feeling that you want in your life. Just as a painter knows what color combinations will give them their desired effect, an Empath can use their emotional states to do what is needed. Recognize what works for you and release what does not.

Get Creative

You don't have to rely on others to achieve an understanding of yourself. It can be difficult when learning how to express your Spirit. All forms of creativity can channel that creative source within you into the physical world. This can help clear your energetic channels and nurture you. This could be through dance, writing, science, art, any avenue that allows for self-expression without judgement.

Multi-Dimensionality

You are amid an energetic evolution within yourself. Practice letting go of that which overwhelms you, confuses you or causes you anxiety while you are discovering how to navigate this new world unfolding before you. As an Empath, you may be used to walking along a multidimensional path which is essentially realizing multiple forms of energy enter your space at the same time and being able to tell them apart.

Strengthen your Abilities

In developing strengths and abilities, you will naturally form a deeper connection to the people around you and the Earth. On your journey, you can strengthen your abilities using some of the methods we've discussed. Below is a recap of those methods and activities that will provide the strength you need as a base for your energy work.

Gratitude- Expressing your gratitude every morning will increase the positive energy in your life. This keeps you focused on the present instead of wasting your energy.

Meditation- When you are moving through your normal workflow or daily life, stop and perform a quick 2- or 3-

minute meditation focused on your Heart Energy. This can bring you back into your personal power when you start to feel overwhelmed. This puts you in charge of your emotional state.

Build your Intuition-Practice using your Intuition when it comes to letting new people into your inner circle. Use Intuition to feel out when energies increase or decrease around certain people.

Self-Love- Read positive affirmations out loud. Use your compassion to help others and feel the capacity you have for empathy grow. Take time to experience your passions and joy. Remember that you are attuned to the energy of life and there is so much to be grateful for because of it.

Remember to celebrate your progress. Those times where you listen to your intuition or assert your boundaries, take a moment to be grateful for the process. It may take time and you may revert to your old ways of being but when you treat yourself with compassion you can learn to trust yourself.

Distance Yourself

Move away from whatever is triggering negative feelings for you. Create that distance between problematic people and situations that is necessary for you to have the space you need to clear or process that energy. You can do this without offending people but be sure that you are honoring yourself first and foremost. Because physical contact increases your empathic response, you want to find out what distance is comfortable for you with each person and situation you come across.

Beware of Negativity

It's possible to go so deep into negative emotions that you feel trapped inside of them. This doesn't mean to ignore them or discount them but to moderate your exposure to them. Always keep back a part of yourself that does not get involved. If the object is not at hand or if you have seen a warning sign you should do something before this happens. Dwelling on negative will do nothing but cause you to isolate yourself and become filled with despair that might not have even originated with you.

Set limitations and boundaries for yourself. If you don't feel like doing something, then don't. It's okay to say No. Remember that "No" is a complete sentence. You don't have to justify why you are saying No to anyone. You don't have to engage any further. This can be huge for managing your energies.

Remember, this does get easier. Your life will probably look quite different in 6-12 months from now. When you start to develop your energies, you will find that you enjoy your empathic gifts and what they can do for you and others.

Strengthen your Abilities

Manage These Gifts

- Smudge your space with sage or other ceremonial herbs to literally change the vibrational energy. Clear any existing energies in a space before turning inward.

- Bathe using sea salts or Himalayan salts that will pull negative ions out of your body and rejuvenate you.

- Collect crystals that deflect energy. Carry these crystals that project their energy outward and use them to create a shield of protection around you.

- Investigate Reiki and other healing treatments such

a therapeutic massage, acupuncture, and Pressure Point therapies.

- Practice "pulling" your aura in closer to your body before you walk out your door and into the world.

Transmutation

When you pick up on an emotion or energy that you know is coming form outside of you than you should transmute it. Simply imagine that the emotion is transformed into a different, higher vibration emotion, or even dissolving into no emotion at all and then send it back out into the Universe. This is easier when dealing with other people's emotions but can be done with our own as well.

We become entangled with everyone that we share emotions with, and we will be able to feel a lifting of their emotion once that emotional energy has been transmuted. The other person may not even realize what has happened, but they will usually feel a difference. This is a gift that you have as an Empath, and it's probably the most important one for healing yourself and others. Embrace this power you must transmute the energies that are coming into your life. Use transmutation to create good.

. . .

Hone your Empathic abilities by concentrating on keeping emotions in your heart. Keep a positive emotion in your heart to nurture your intuition. Remember that every minute that you spend focusing on positive emotion is valuable. This will come in handy the next time you encounter negative energies. You can simply access that emotion held in your heart space to create an energetic barrier that those negative vibes cannot permeate.

11

Additional Strategies for Those
with Empathic Natures

As an Empath, you must suspend your acceptance of the world as you know it. Allow yourself to contemplate the possibility of all the different ways that you can find yourself in this world. Think about all the ways that you can create and reinvent yourself. Using our empathic appreciation for other's experiences we can practice radical empathy. This means that we can understand those experiences without ever questioning our commonality.

Our most efficient technique for honoring our Empathic gift is positive speaking through positive thinking. This includes the positive verbal expression of ideas. It's the Empath's inward communicative thinking and feeling that directly influences the way their subconscious mind processes their needs. For example, creating a mediated emotional state that you can share with someone. It means having someone "see the silver lining' even through vast darkness. This includes having a positive environment and making sure everyone is comfortable for a more favorable outcome.

Practice these strategies for truly embracing your Empathic gifts and sensitivities. Develop your own and use them to create space for yourself and others.

Listen with passion

Use visual cues to show a person that you're not only listening to them but are hearing what they have to say. If required to respond, an Empath should keep their speech positive and keep all responses brief. Checking in by asking "why do you feel this way" or "what do you know about?" ensures that you are getting to the bottom on a situation or emotional state of a person.

Create Your Space

Maintain your spiritual energy and create your own personal energy stations at home and work. This includes pictures, crystals that you resonate with, and anything that centers you. Create a circle of safety for yourself with your space. Summon your own inner power to create a personalized visualization for yourself. Doing so will allow you to focus easier. If you are able, set up a space or room that is used only for meditation and energy work. Look into singing bowls and other sounds or music that will create the atmosphere you need.

Reduce your Need to Please

Reclaim your sovereignty over your body. Look beneath the surface to find why you have the need of "why do you need to please." Why are you hyper agreeable? Do you feel the need to do so? What's the motivation behind this feeling? Once you understand the internal motivations driving this need to please, you can start to chart a path to wellbeing. The need to please typically stems from underlying fears. The fear of being unloved. Of being inconsequential. Without having worth or significance. This fear can be dealt with by perceiving needs of others and reaching out assertively even militantly to makes sure others needs are met. The payoff is the feeling of exhilaration, the feeling of connection and joy and a boost to the sense of self. The need to please keeps perpetuating this fear.

Think about what gives you worth outside of this ability? You must realize that you *give* because you have worth. Not that you gain worth through giving. This distinction is huge for Empaths. Understanding the motivation behind your behaviors is the first step. This requires self-exploration. Identify patterns that may have started even in childhood, and consistently perform a very complex examination of self.

. . .

Be Vulnerable

In regard to increasing your sensitivities, this vulnerability can manifest as a fear of being without protection. As an Empath having different energy, this fear says if you don't give or please or be agreeable or going along with others agenda that you might be a threat. This could lead you to perceive that others will withdraw their protection and/or support. There can be a lot of anxiety under the mask of the Empath. Fear of retribution or being blamed if things go wrong. There is a fear of losing security so Empaths will go along to get along.

When there are those with predatory personalities both types of fear can be triggered. Some strategies to battle this would be to gain insight into the futility of gaining love by continuously giving. Insight into the need to give. On what levels do you need to get? Place the foundation of your worth in a solid position. Increase your insight and aware-ness and actively take steps to stop yourself from reaching out reflexively to satisfy other's needs.

Assert Yourself

Reclaim your own sense of your internal authority and your capacity to deal with the world and authority figures. You possess an internal reservoir of protection. You don't have to be agreeable in exchange for validation. Find and practice Assertion exercises. Work on increasing your personal power and authority.

Get in tune with your ebbs and flows of energy throughout the day. Are you chemically sensitive? What personal care products are you using and are they placing any burden on your body?

Know yourself, deeply. Know your own mind. Know your emotional states and be prepared to access that information on the fly.

Cleansing the Etheric body

Metaphysically clean out all the vibes, and energies that are not your own from time to time. This can stop stress from building and building and reaching a maximum capacity limit. If you aren't regularly cleaning this energy out you can become withdrawn, quiet, depressed, neurotic, even narcissistic. You can do this by grounding, meditating, clearing chakras, etc.

Affirmations for Empaths

Anything that you repeatedly think or say to yourself is essentially an Affirmation. Your habitual thinking patterns become your beliefs. You want to make sure that you are feeding your mind positivity. Pay attention to those thoughts that fill your days so that you can eliminate that which does not serve you.

When you hang on to negative feelings you are creating a space for them to flourish. When you are actively manifesting things into your life you must take care to affirm what you do want to create. Keep in mind that simply saying an affirmation is only one part of the process. Choosing to think those thoughts that keep you feeling good is essential for the information you are affirming.

You can write your own affirmations by simply describing things that you want to experience or have. Write about them in the present tense, such as "I am healthy", and "I am loved." Be sure to remove any works like want or need from affirmations as they reaffirm the fact that you don't yet have them which can work against the power of manifestation. You need to affirm that feeling of already having that which you desire. For example, if you want and need a new house you could word it as "I love my new house, I'm grateful for living in my dream home."

Take note of any negative or low energy words. There is a difference between "I am getting myself out of all debts" and "I am prosperous and wealthy." Just imagine that you've already accomplished your desires and describe yourself in that new light. Create affirmations that use your own way of thinking. Be silly if you need, or as detailed as you want.

Don't set limits to how these things can show up in your life. Once you put yourself into the frame of mind of already having what you're affirming you must allow the universe to figure out the best way to get it to you. Let go of any thoughts around what you think you deserve. Let go of any reservations you have for asking for too much. Your limited beliefs have no weight with the universe.

Affirmations for Setting Boundaries

"I'm not responsible for fixing things for others. There is a lesson in the emotions that others experience. I do not wish to deprive them of this valuable learning with my involvement."

"The feelings of others are not my business. Just because I can feel it doesn't mean that they want me to. I allow others the same privacy that I want and need."

"We are all human, and I must accept people for who they are. I may have the ability to feel their emotions but that doesn't mean that they can read mine."

"This will pass. I can release that which I do not want. I give these feelings back with love."

Affirmations for Empathic Positivity

"I am on the same side as other beings. My commitment to others is including them in a field of empathy."

"I am cared for completely, and fully by the Universe."

"I can position myself to experience harmony with others and maintain harmonious relationships."

"I extend compassionate love to those with hurtful views and opinions."

Affirmations for Self-Care

"I treasure myself and commit to bringing those into my life that value me."

"I seek to find balance with my intuition and emotion so that I can express the spectrum of my sensitivity."

"I will take time to rest and recharge. I will not hide my abilities from others."

"I will listen to my body and it's wisdom. I will find balance."

Affirmations for Love

"My life is full of love."

"My partner and I have a deep understanding."

"I experience loving kindness daily."

"Kindness and Compassion come first."

Remember, you must **feel** your affirmations. Don't repeat them just for the sake of doing so. Learn to associate your emotions and feelings to your affirmations. Be consistent. Practice your new affirmations daily. Start with one or two powerful affirmations and meditate on them for a week or two before changing things up. Make it become a habit. If you set the pace correctly in the beginning, you're more likely to continue with it.

Think about your ideal life. As an Empath, consider how you want to use your abilities in the service of others. What experiences are you looking forward to having? What inter-actions and perceptions do you want to introduce into your existence? Use affirmations however you feel most comfort-able. This might mean one that you repeat daily like a mantra or a dozen that you read and repeat throughout the day. Some people will put an affirmation of gratitude on their mirror so that they will repeat it every day before leaving their house. Find what makes you feel good.

Believe that you are achieving, and you will put your full effort into it. Remember you have the potential to rewire the neural pathways in your brain with these affirmations!

. . .

Meditations for Empaths

Meditation is about experiencing the rhythms and depths of the universe. By becoming one with ourselves and life itself can greatly improve the quality of our lives. This can be done by simply stilling the mind by focusing on our breath, a determined focal point, and by observing our thoughts.

This can go a long way when an Empath seeks to center or ground themselves. Calming the mind can have lasting effects, long after the meditation is over. This includes stress relief and an awareness that not many will be able to attain. With a mind that can be overstimulated, it can be a much-needed rest that allows you to focus on the present.

When starting out try to dedicate at least 15 minutes to practice meditation exercises. Try searching for guided meditations for Empaths online. While you don't need anything other than a quiet space and a few minutes, having a guided meditation that focuses on a need can be extremely helpful.

Get comfortable and focus on your breathing. Many meditation exercises will begin with at least a few minutes of deep breathing where you focus on filling your lungs completely and exhaling while counting or saying certain words that make you focus on taking full, complete breaths. Breathe through your diaphragm.

Many guided meditations will essentially be an adventure in visualization. Most will include an orb of light coming towards you or coming out of you. Sometimes it can be helpful to focus on one of your affirmations so that when you notice any other thoughts coming through that are resistant to being quickly released, you can focus on that affirmation to pull your focus back to yourself and your breath.

If you are invested in the process, you can see extremely positive results from meditation in a short amount of time. It can help you manage your stress and anxiety by focusing on those experiences from moment-to-moment. Mostly it can help bring you a sense of peace and calm with is crucial for an Empath to incorporate into their daily lives.

Take care of Yourself

Go to bed early. Empaths are notorious for being night owls and for burning the candle from both ends. End any reliance you might have on stimulants to keep yourself going through the day as it can create problems with your sleep cycles. Practice winding down techniques every night. Look into blue light filtering software and limit your screen-time. Regulate your sleep/wake cycle by getting up at the same time every morning consistently.

Take the time that you need for you. That might mean going solo on dates or when searching out new places. You don't necessarily have to interact with new energies but be sure to spend time doing things for yourself. You can get to know yourself on an entirely different level by practicing self-love. Read a book, play music, do the things that you love to do. Honor yourself where you are at in your journey. Recoup, regroup, an refuel yourself before you go back out into the world again.

Eat Breakfast

Eating breakfast that has enough protein can help give you the energy needed just to go out in public. It can be easier to simply skip eating breakfast and rely on caffeine, but that dependency will be less effective the more you do it. It can result in high levels of cortisol, crashing from sugar and caffeine, etc. Focus on high-quality protein and complex carbohydrates to stabilize your blood sugars and give you natural energy for your energy work. Be careful not to mask your true fatigue levels and of course, stay hydrated.

Lower your Toxicity

As Empaths we must reconcile the fact that we can be the emotional vampires to other people sometimes. It's part of being human but we can catch ourselves and use our aware-ness to stop the behavior in its tracks. Do not be a toxic influence on others. Use your positive energy to uplift the people around you. If you find that you or anyone else is being a drama queen, a chronic complainer or being passive aggressive simply address it lovingly and work to understand the person and the situation.

· · ·

Use Your Gifts

You are a natural healer and you can use these abilities by letting your energy flow. You have access to your inner guidance on a heightened level. Connect to this source energy and use it! This journey will be worth all the effort that you put into it.

Conclusion

Congratulations on making it through to the end of Empath: Empowering Highly Sensitive People - Maximizing your Potential and Self-Awareness! We hope that it was able to provide you with the information you were seeking regarding identifying yourself as an Empath. By applying the techniques for self-awareness and energy awareness found in this book you should be able to start embracing your Empathic gifts and create a significant change in the way you interact with the world.

By understanding that you are a co-creator in the universe and that your gifts reach far beyond the common experience you can begin to heal yourself, and in turn, others. Remember that you must be willing to take responsibility for your own thoughts, emotions, and actions before you can begin to understand the motivation and energies of others.

Once you have identified what type of Empath you are, and what sensitivities you'd like to work on, you can begin to work on centering and grounding yourself as a form of protection and self-development.

Recognize those areas where you might be projecting your own energy onto others. Check yourself for narcissistic and co-dependent behaviors that we can pick up from others and hold on to. Use the information regarding the Science behind Empathy to understand how and why you can experience emotions in the way that you can. Take note of the questions you have that there may not be answers to quite yet.

You should have a better understanding of where emotions originate in each of us, and how negative associations can be such a part of our being that we don't even realize they are there. Use your Intuition as an Empath to identify and release such emotions from your state of being and help others to transmute their energies into something more positive. Remember to allow yourself the space you need to discover how much exposure you can handle at first.

Practice visualization and grounding techniques to block out the unwanted emotions of others and pay attention to the types of energy you surround yourself with. Take the time you need to work on yourself and raise your vibration. Use affirmations and meditations to keep yourself centered and focused on the loving energy that surrounds us.

When we are willing to acknowledge the work that we must do on ourselves and deal with our feelings and emotions honestly, we open ourselves up to the healing nature of the Empath. Listen to your mind and body to give you the information you need on this journey. Remember to breathe and create the boundaries you need to feel secure and determined. Embrace this paradigm shift and expansion of being. Find and take comfort in a community that holds space for you and accepts your sensitivities as the most special part about your existence in the present moment.

Finally, cultivate a culture of peace both within yourself and the world around you. Embrace the challenges that you are sure to face on this journey. Be well!

CPSIA information can be obtained
at www.ICGtesting.com
Printed in the USA
LVHW022119180520
655844LV00003B/314